Which? way to make soft furnishings

Which? way to make soft furnishings

Consumers' Association and Hodder & Stoughton

First published in 1983 in Great Britain by
Consumers' Association
14 Buckingham Street, London WC2N 6DS
and Hodder & Stoughton
47 Bedford Square, London WC1B 3DP

First reprint 1986
Second reprint 1987

Compiled by David Mason

Designed by Bridget Morley and Sue Rawkins
Illustrations by Carole Johnson, Anne Howard,
Ann Savage, Tony Lodge, Shirley Willis
Cover photograph by Philip Dowell
Sofa cover by Joanna Willis Fleming

Printed and bound in Great Britain
by Butler & Tanner Ltd, Frome and London

ISBN 0 340 33167 4

Acknowledgements for their help to
Annabel Bool and Margaret Colvin

Contents

Introduction

Soft furnishing is a craft and, as with all crafts, it is the individual character of an article that gives it quality and value. Few professionals can spare the time that such individuality needs if they are to make an adequate living, but someone at home can afford to give greater care and attention in order to create a beautiful object. This book demonstrates that it is not beyond the scope of most people's skills to make soft-furnished articles which match the best available in terms of professional workmanship, but which also carry the individual mark of the person who made them.

We have included a spectrum of projects ranging in size from sumptuous bed-hangings to a simple egg cosy. The large items are not invariably the most difficult – some of the curtains and bedspreads are quite straightforward – and the small items not always quick and easy, particularly if they involve extra decorative stages. But in general many of the projects are much easier than they might appear. Table linen and cushions are two of the most rewarding areas, particularly for sewing novices, since they are open to the most individual approaches without too great an outlay of either time or money.

Fabric is an expensive commodity and the more complex, beautiful and useful it is, the more expensive it becomes. In soft furnishing a great deal of material can be involved, but even so it is wise to spend as much as you can afford since good quality will pay off in longevity and continuing good looks. One of the main advantages of doing the work yourself is that it may allow you to choose a more extravagant fabric.

The skills required are relatively basic – the standard stitches and techniques are explained at the back of the book. You need of course to be able to handle a needle and thread and a pair of scissors. Don't tackle soft furnishing in a confined space. A large expanse of floor is probably one of the most useful things to have, second only to a sewing machine. As with dressmaking, it is best to have the ironing-board up all the time while you work so that there is no temptation *not* to press seams as you go along. Assemble all the tools and equipment before you start so that you don't suddenly realise that you lack something absolutely vital just as you come to a tricky bit.

Special techniques such as piping edges, lockstitching linings to curtains, and lampshade-making are described in the body of the book where they are immediately relevant. Similarly, those that fit more into the realms of upholstery are explained in context. If you become lured by the idea of upholstery, see this book's companion volume, *Which? way to repair and restore furniture*.

Other cardinal rules for a professional article: plan your scheme and allow a lot of time for wandering round furniture shops and fabric departments as well as browsing through magazines; don't skimp at the measuring stages; and when you do start cutting, fitting and sewing, allow enough time for each session so that you can enjoy the sense of accomplishment that makes soft furnishing such a satisfying and creative occupation.

Curtains and blinds

Few skills are more valuable in your home than the ability to make your own curtains. Almost every room needs them. They serve several purposes: in the day they prevent windows looking stark and bare and at night they shut out the rest of the world and give a room an atmosphere of warmth and cosiness. And, most important in times of high energy costs, they can be made to form an effective insulation layer, keeping the heat inside the house and cutting out draughts.

They have a critical influence on the appearance of the room. If the windows are large, the curtains can be made full length, and if the windows are small, the curtains can be made small. In general, a window's position and proportions in relation to the whole room can be enhanced or disguised appropriately. If the

room is quite dark, don't cut out more light than you need. If there is a radiator beneath the window, floor-length curtains may prevent the heat coming into the room efficiently when they are closed.

Whatever their size, curtains tend to dominate a room. A pair of full-length curtains with a shaped pelmet can suggest the atmosphere of a large country house. If you are designing a room to use as an office, simple uncluttered curtains with an unfussy pattern and heading will cause minimum distraction.

If you choose a fabric which is in harmony with the other decorations and furnishings in the room, the curtains will have a calming influence. You might even consider having wallpaper and curtain fabric matching other items in the room. Or, for a dramatic

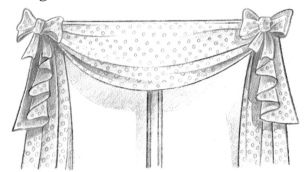

effect, choose a fabric with a bold design (though large patterns are uneconomical because you will have to buy extra in order to match up the pattern).

The type of fabric itself can have a great influence on the character and style of a room. The subtle light-and-shade effect of plain velvet can generate a feeling of opulence. A colourful cotton print will cheer up an otherwise dingy space.

When choosing the fabric bear in mind that it should be hard-wearing and easy to clean. Towelling and plastic-coated fabrics would be practical choices for a kitchen or bathroom. In other rooms, more expensive fabrics need lining for protection from sunlight as well as for enhancing their looks (silk rots in sunlight). Some upholstery fabrics are too heavy and don't drape well, and even those heavy fabrics that *are* suitable (furnishing velvet, for instance) might have to be rejected if their bulk will cut down light when they are drawn back.

Most curtains benefit from being lined. The lining helps to keep the curtain clean, acts as an insulator against the cold and noise, looks neater from the outside of the house than the reverse side of the curtain fabric, and helps to stop the curtain fabric fading by taking the full impact of any direct sunlight. Choose lining fabric in a colour to match the curtain fabric, or opt for an orthodox white, beige or cream. Coloured linings will show fading before pale ones, and may show through and affect the curtain adversely.

You can also add interlining. Lined-and-interlined curtains are only slightly more difficult to make than lined-only curtains, and are worth the extra expense. The interlining is a layer of cotton-based or synthetic fabric between the lining and the curtain. Correctly fitted, it gives the edges of the curtain a thickness and 'roll' that lends a touch of luxury to even the most modest fabrics and, perhaps more importantly, it forms an even more effective insulation barrier. Make sure that the curtain fabric, lining and interlining are all compatible in terms of washing or dry-cleaning.

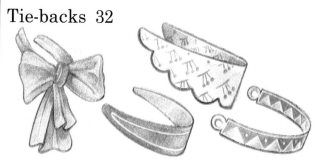

Tracks and fittings

The type of track you choose will affect the appearance of the curtains, and with it the room. There is a bewildering array of curtain track fittings and hanging systems, and the manufacturers change their ranges often enough to make it unwise to try to cover the subject comprehensively here. The best way to choose a track is to study the range available.

Your choice will depend on your decorating scheme and on the type of heading (see below). These will dictate the style and material of the track: it might be aluminium, plastic, brass, brass-plated metal, or wood. You might prefer a pole which would look elegant in some period settings, especially when used to carry full-length curtains in a large room. If you prefer the convenience of a track but the appearance of a pole, there is available a half-section pole which conceals a track mechanism.

If you are using a pelmet, a board will probably be essential to carry the weight (page 22), but a valance can be carried on a curtain track.

Tracks are available that can be bent to follow the contours of the area, such as a bay or dormer window. For a dormer window, a continuation of the track round the sides allows you to draw the curtain completely away from the window in order to let in as much light as possible.

Net curtains sometimes have different fittings (see page 29).

If you prefer detachable linings, you may find it useful to instal the type of track which takes a special kind of hooked glider on which you can hang both the curtain and the lining.

Most manufacturers make a system for opening and closing the curtains with a single pulled cord which will save the fabric from handling. You should also consider this if the curtains are very tall or heavy. It is possible to instal an electrically operated opening-and-closing system.

A track extending round to the sides of a dormer window enables the curtains to be drawn right back to let as much light into the room as possible.

If you prefer to close and open the curtains by hand you can fit rods to the inner edge hooks to avoid handling and possibly soiling the curtain fabric itself. Or you can fit a tasselled draw cord.

Heading tape

You will need to decide exactly which type of heading tape you want to use, and calculate the length. It is possible to make your own headings but there are enough good manufactured tapes for this to be unnecessary. If you are planning to make several curtains with the same heading, you might feel it worth investing in a full roll of the particular tape.

These are the main types of heading tapes in general use (fig 1 overleaf):

Standard tape draws the curtain up into a simple gather. It produces a shallow heading and can be used with an exposed track but is generally more suitable for use with pelmets. It takes standard curtain hooks, which should be inserted every 8 cm for medium-weight curtains. You will need twice the track width of both tape and fabric.

Standard heading tape

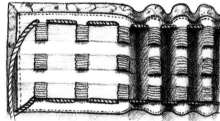
Pencil pleat tape

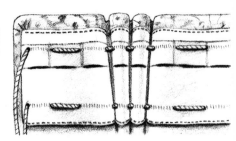
Triple pleat tape

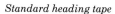

1 These are three of the most usual types of heading tape. Pencil pleats give the cleanest effect if you are not having a pelmet. All types take ordinary curtain hooks.

Pencil pleat tape is the most straightforward and satisfactory type of decorative tape when there is no pelmet. It draws up into a tidy series of tight pleats approximately the thickness of a pencil, and takes standard hooks. Versions such as Rufflette Regis tape are stiffened to give a firm crisp heading, and an extra deep version (14 cm) is available to give a well-proportioned heading for floor-length curtains. Special versions of pencil pleating tape are available for net and sheer curtains. Use $2\frac{1}{2}$ times the track width for standard curtains, twice the track width for the deeper heading tape, and up to three times the track width for net curtains.

Triple pleat tape gives the effect of a group of three pinched pleats without the need for long-pronged hooks. Drawing up the strings produces spaced triple pleats. It is available in a variety of depths – 14 cm, 9 cm and 4 cm – buy any of these to twice the track width.

Cartridge pleat tape This heading produces a well-rolled pleat effect and evenly hanging curtains below the heading. Use the hooks recommended by the manufacturer. You will need twice the track width.

Lining tape is used for detachable linings and is hung on the curtain hooks (see Making linings on page 18).

Net heading tapes A wide range is available to give approximately the same choice of heading styles as on curtains: pencil pleats, plain gathers, pinch and triple pleats, and cylindrical pleats like the cartridge pleat.

Other equipment

Like good clothes, curtains look infinitely better if they are sewn by hand, and indeed all the hems on the curtains described here are hand-sewn, but a sewing machine is necessary for applying the heading to the curtains, taking up the hems on the linings, joining widths of fabric, and other otherwise tedious jobs.

You will need pins, needles, synthetic sewing thread in a colour to match the curtain fabric, and enough hooks to fit the rings appropriate to the length of track – your supplier will tell you what you need. If you haven't already got a pair of scissors it is worth investing in the best pair of dressmaking scissors you can afford (this applies to any of the projects in this book). Modern scissors in a lightweight alloy with cheerfully coloured (and easily located) plastic handles are light and quick to use and unlikely to make your thumb joint ache. The advantage of the heavy steel scissors that tailors use is that you can sharpen them yourself.

An iron and ironing-board, and a fabric tape measure are also necessary. You will find the job of making hems and seams easier if you have a short ruler – a cheap wooden school one will do the job. If you find it unwieldy, cut it in half.

You will almost certainly not have the one tool that a professional curtain-maker would regard as essential. A commercial workroom will be nearly filled by a vast table, on which a curtain can be laid out at full length for measuring. You will have to make do with the floor or as big a table as possible with a protective blanket laid on it.

Measuring the window

The first job is to measure up for the curtains. Take a notebook and pencil to the window, together with a rule and a chair or stepladder for standing on. A metre stick would be a help but equally good, and more likely to be found in your household tool kit, is an extending steel rule. (All measurements here are metric, but there is a conversion chart on page 129.)

Sketch a picture of the window on your notepad (fig 2). Now determine how far on each side, and above and below, the curtain should extend. First the height above, which will be where the track will fit. If the window is extremely small, 8 cm will be sufficient. If the window is slightly larger, say one metre or more in depth, then a distance of 12 cm will be approximately right for the position of the track.

Now determine the finished width of the track (don't bother with the width of the window). Remember that if the window is wide you will need more space at each side for containing the curtain when it is drawn back. If you have chosen to fit the track 12 cm above the window, then a distance of 12 cm on each side will be appropriate. If the window is smaller, and the track lower, it should extend less at the sides.

Lastly work out the length of the curtain. Put a small pencil mark on the wall below the sill at the point where you think the bottom of the

2 Sketch a picture of the window on your notepad and decide how far above, below and to each side the curtains are to extend. These are the crucial measurements, not those of the window frame itself.

curtain should hang. Again, 12 cm or a little more below the window will be about right. If the curtains are to hang in a recess let them fall to about 1 cm above the recess. Floor-length curtains should hang about 1 cm above the floor.

Fitting the track

Now fit your track, following the manufacturer's instructions. Hang a track ring or glider in the appropriate groove and measure from the bottom of the ring down to the mark on the wall showing the bottom of the curtain. This is known as the 'hook drop'. If you are making curtains to extend right to the floor or the sill, you will need to make sure this measurement is absolutely accurate.

Estimating the fabric

Now you can calculate the width of material to buy. Generally, you should aim for the width of material to be twice the length of the track. When the curtains are closed, they will then fall into pleasant folds. If you have less than this double width, the curtains will look flat and skimped. If you have more, they may not hang comfortably when drawn back off the window.

Again, this is not a precise rule, and a little more or less will not make much difference. For a small window, you need to have only one width of material in each curtain. So, assuming the track is 120 cm wide, that is the width of material to choose (material is available in other widths). If your window is very narrow, say only 50 or 60 cm, it would be better to use only one small curtain to cover it, hung to one side and using the widest fabric available. If it is over about 60 cm, choose the narrower width of fabric, and make one curtain for each side of the window.

You can now calculate the length required. Recall your hook drop measurement. You will have to add two other measurements. One is for a hem at the bottom of the curtain: we recommend a double hem, so add 12 cm. The other is for the heading at the top. This is the most interesting part of the curtain. It is structurally important because it carries the hooks that hold up the curtain, it covers the track when the curtains are closed, and it is also an important part of the decoration. For this small curtain a simple pencil pleat will be appropriate. To form this type of heading, you should add 7.5 cm to the length. Add a further 15 cm to the total length so that you can square off the material in case it gets cut badly in the shop.

So the formula (in centimetres) for working out the amount of material to buy for a simple pair of curtains with no widths joined is:

$$
\begin{array}{rl}
\text{Hook drop } (say) & 210 \\
& +12 \quad (hem) \\
& +\ 7.5\ (heading*) \\
\hline
= & 229.5 \\
& \times\ 2 \quad (for\ 2\ curtains) \\
\hline
= & 459 \\
& +15 \quad (to\ offset\ shop's \\
& \qquad\quad possibly\ bad\ cutting) \\
\hline
\text{Total } = & 474 \quad (cm) \\
\hline
\end{array}
$$

this is for pencil pleats – other heading tapes may need more or less

Round the total up to the nearest quarter of a metre or other amount that the shop is willing to sell you.

If the material has a pattern with a repeat, add on the length of the repeat to your calculations for each curtain since you will have to cut the two pieces to match. Bear in mind that the bottom of the pattern repeat should occur at the foot of the curtains (after the hem is taken up).

If you have to join widths because a single width of fabric won't be enough, consider the material you are using. As a general rule, light curtains need a greater width than heavy ones. Also, take into account the heading you have chosen: simple gathered headings need about $1\frac{1}{2}$ times the width of the track, pinch pleats need $2-2\frac{1}{2}$ times that width, and pencil pleats and various other headings up to three times the width of the track. It is false economy to skimp on the fullness as the curtains will look wrong.

If the curtains are to overlap in the middle when drawn, add on 15 cm to each curtain's width. Add a further 5 cm for each side hem (20 cm). This will give you the total width of curtaining across the window. Divide that total by the width of the fabric on the roll, and round the answer up to the next whole figure: this is the total number of widths you will need.

Then in order to arrive at the amount of material to buy, multiply the total length of the curtain (including hem and heading but not allowing extra at this stage for a possible cutting error in the shop) by the total number of widths needed.

Add on the depth of any pattern repeat times the total number of widths, and round up the figure to the next half-metre to allow for cutting errors in the shop and for possible shrinkage later.

Your total requirements will be increased if you plan to make a pelmet, valance and/or fabric tie-backs – see pages 23, 26 and 33 for guidance on how to work out your extra requirements.

Cutting the fabric

Spread out the fabric on your table or floor. You need first of all to establish a straight line across one end at right angles to the selvedges. All the lengths of fabric must be cut from this line – otherwise the curtains will not hang properly. The preferable way to do this is to pull a thread from across the weave if it is a fairly loose-woven fabric. If the fabric is printed linen or chintz you

1 *A half-repeat on a fabric with a bold design doesn't look so obvious at the top of the curtain where it will be obscured in the heading.*

are unlikely to be able to do this as the grain tends to shift during the printing process, so line the fabric up with the end of the table to give you a right angle or devise some other accurate way of finding the angle (a set square would be ideal).

If the fabric is patterned, the curtains will look best if the pattern repeat coincides with the bottom of the curtain after the hem has been taken up. A half-repeat doesn't look so obvious at the top of the curtain where it will be obscured in the heading (fig 1). So cut the lengths of fabric starting 12 cm (the total amount needed to form the hem) below the bottom of a repeat.

As with all soft furnishing, it is wise to follow the maxim 'Measure twice, cut once'. Refer to the measurements list and mark off the cutting points with a couple of pins. Check that the measurements still hold good before you cut. As you cut off each length, mark what will be the top with dressmaker's chalk, pins or a tailor's tack. This is especially important for a fabric with a pile or nap such as velvet, when all the pieces must run in the same direction – if the pile runs downwards you can dust the curtains more easily but they will look more opulent if the pile runs upwards.

Joining widths of fabric

If you have to join widths, you would do well to lay out the pieces in front of the window at this stage to make sure that you get all the parts in the right places. Join the widths symmetrically (fig 2). It looks better if you arrange the seams to fall towards the outer edges of the curtain.

When you have laid out the pieces, snip off a small triangle from the corners to show which piece joins up with which other piece. Then lay the parts out, right side to right side, with the edges in line. Pin them together, starting at the bottom, 1 cm in from the selvedge, and with the pins every 10 cm or so parallel to the selvedges. Snip the selvedges to release the tension (fig 3).

2 *Make sure that any pattern on joined widths matches up. Bear this in mind right from the beginning and buy enough fabric to allow the leeway to do this.*

3 *To join widths of fabric, pin them right sides together, edges level. The pins should run parallel to the selvedge. Snip the selvedges all along to release any tension.*

Sew along the line of the pins, removing them as you go. If you have pinned from the bottom, sew from the top. Alternatively, you can put the two pieces straight into the sewing machine, using the sewing foot as a guide to get the sewing line a constant distance from the selvedge. Make an ordinary flat seam in either case.

Joining widths of patterned fabric introduces an additional complication. In a pattern with a strongly repeated motif, you may find that half of one motif is likely to line up with a full motif which would look wrong. You may find that you have to lose up to almost an entire pattern repeat on each curtain. If you *have* chosen a heavily patterned fabric, however, cut your first two main lengths as explained above. Then move the next part up and down against one of the lengths to work out the match. Rather than having a full width plus a part-width you may find the answer is to have two part-widths which won't interfere with the pattern. It will be a case of trial and error in deciding where the centre seam will be so that the pattern will look the least disturbed, and you will need at the same time to bear in mind where the side hems will occur after joining the cut widths together. Although it is

time-consuming, it is advisable to tack along the seam after pinning it, before you sew. This seam should be a run-and-fell one which will have the effect of neatening the cut edges. This exercise is tricky and needs lots of concentration.

Making up the curtains

With the lengths accurately cut and any widths joined, you can now start making the curtains. Lay one curtain out on the ironing board, wrong side up, with the bottom edge facing you. Starting at one of the bottom corners measure with a wooden ruler 12 cm from the bottom. Turn the fabric up so that the wrong sides are together and press in a crease with the iron at a fairly cool setting. Continue along the bottom, measuring at close intervals for accuracy. That crease will form the bottom edge of the finished curtain. Any pattern should match all along the hem line.

Open out the fold. Work your way once more across the fabric with the iron, but this time fold the bottom hem in half, turning the raw edge up as accurately as possible to meet the fold you have just made. Turn the fabric up once more at the first crease, and you will have a neat double

1 *Turning up the curtain hem: wrong sides together, press in a crease 12 cm from the bottom. This will be the bottom edge of the curtain. Then open out the fold, turn the raw edge up to meet the crease, and press in a second crease. Fold up again along the first crease to make a double 6 cm hem. Pin along the top before slipstitching the hem in place.*

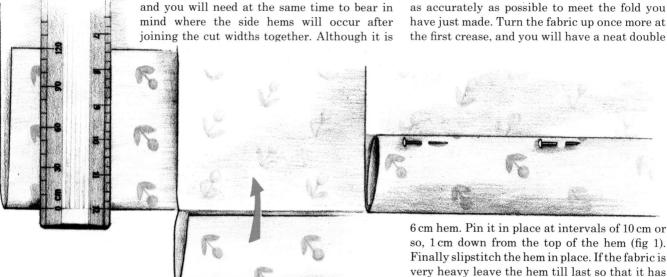

6 cm hem. Pin it in place at intervals of 10 cm or so, 1 cm down from the top of the hem (fig 1). Finally slipstitch the hem in place. If the fabric is very heavy leave the hem till last so that it has time to hang properly (see page 17).

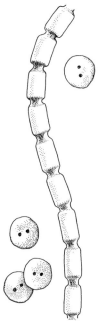

2 *Curtain weights to thread through the hem or sew into the hem corners.*

3 *The inner edge of the curtain: lift up the overhang of the heading tape and pull out the cords underneath from the first three slots. Tie the ends securely, then fold under and pin the tape so that the knot is hidden.*

Sew the sides next. It is preferable to do them after the hem so that the edge of the bottom hem is hidden at the sides of the curtain. First fold the material in by 4 cm and press it. If you keep the iron fairly cool, you can use the iron to hold the material in position while you ease it out taut with your left hand, and measure it with your right. Move the iron along to put in the crease.

Go back to the beginning, and turn the material in to make the double thickness. This time do not fold the hem in half, but turn it in by 1.5 cm, leaving a side hem of 2.5 cm. Press it, pin it in place, then hand-sew it.

Weights

Some fabrics hang better if they are weighted at the bottom. A good stockist will carry a range of at least three grades of flexible weights. The correct grade to use will depend on the type of fabric and the curtain length. As a general rule use 25 g per metre weights for net curtains, 70 g per metre for lightweight fabrics, and 150 g per metre for heavy fabrics. Sew the sides of the curtains first; then turn up the hem and fold up and press in mitred corners. If you are using those weights that look like a string of sausages, handstitch along the hem, thread the weights through with the help of a safety-pin, and then close up the mitred edges. Stitch invisibly round the weights at intervals to secure them. Sew the coin type of weights in the corners.

Preparing the heading

Lay one curtain wrong side up on your table or floor. Refer to your notes and recall the hook drop that you measured, and add the width of the heading tape. On the flat surface, start marking off this new measurement from the bottom of the curtain. Providing you have cut and measured everything squarely at all preceding stages, you will have a consistent length for the whole curtain. (You might think it would be easier to measure from the top down to the hook, but it is safer to do that afterwards, as a double-check.)

When you have marked off the hook drop plus the measurement of the heading, fold the fabric along this point and press it flat, just as you did the bottom hem. At this stage you may want to consider adding a certain crispness to the heading. This is done by ironing on or sewing a band of Vilene or other heavyweight interfacing under the fold of the heading, the width of the curtain and about 5 cm deep.

Next you need to fix the heading tape to the curtain 2 cm down from the top (1 cm for pencil pleats). It is best not to risk getting this right by eye, so go across the fabric with the wooden ruler inserting pins parallel to the top edge at the 2 cm mark. Leave an overhang of 2.5 cm at each side. There are two loose strings running through the tape. You need to make them secure because if they ever come loose, you will have to re-make the heading of your curtain.

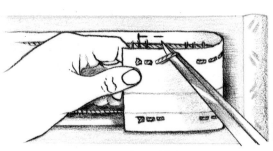

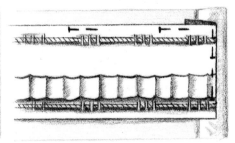

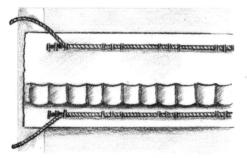 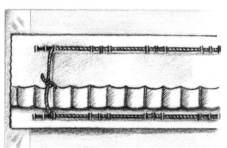 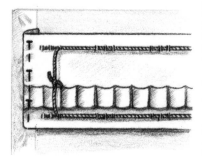

1 *The outer edge of the curtain: pull out the cords from the overhang through the top of the tape and knot them. Fold the tape under and pin it in place. At this edge the cords need to be accessible in order to draw them up.*

First work out which is the inner edge of your curtain – that is, the edge that will be at the centre of the window. Lift the end of the tape up to expose the underside and count back three of the small slots through which the cord runs. Pull the cord out of those three slots with the points of your scissors. Tie the two ends together securely on the underside. Fold the end of the tape under, with the knot lying underneath so that the edge of the tape lies just within the edge of the curtain (fig 3 on page 15). Pin it in place.

At the outer edge of the curtain again pull out the string as far as the third hole along, but this time pull it out through the front of the tape. Knot the ends of the two cords together, but not too close to the tape. You simply need to stop the cords working their way out of the tape. Fold the tape under, just in from the edge of the curtain, and pin it in place (fig 1).

You will have to sew the tape to the heading, perfectly flat, along both its top and bottom edges, and secure it at the ends. The best way is to machine sew along the top, turn at the corner, and machine down the end of the tape. Cut the

thread. Move the material back in the machine to start again on the top, stitching 2.5 cm in from the end. Sew along the top 2.5 cm distance to the corner, turn and sew down the end, turn again and sew right across the curtain to the opposite side, turn the material again, and sew up the opposite end to the top (fig 2). Sewing in the same direction along the two long sides prevents the fabric or the heading pulling.

All you have to do now to finish the curtain is gather it up to form the pleats. Refer to the track measurement and halve it. The curtain will have to cover this half-length. Now add 10 cm to the measurement so that the two curtains will meet comfortably in the middle without straining.

You need to gather up the curtain on the cord to the right length. If you have no one to help you, hook the looser knot in the cord (the one you tied second) over a door-knob and pull the heading tape along the taut cord. Some curtain-makers recommend drawing the heading tape as tight as possible on the string, then letting it out to the right length. Whichever way suits you, the pleats must be crisp and evenly formed.

2 *The best way to ensure that the heading will lie flat is to machine along its edges in the directions indicated. Starting 2.5 cm in from one end will give the greatest strength.*

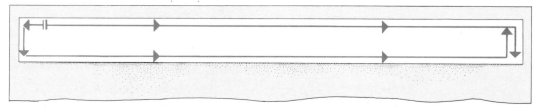

When you have the heading gathered to the right length, tie up the loose cord into a neat coil. Do not cut it off or knot it: when you take the curtains down for washing or cleaning, you will have to flatten the heading.

You could buy a small plastic cord-tidy for coiling the loose ends of the cord, or you could wind the ends into a figure-of-eight over your fingers to make a neat bundle.

Fit the hooks at regular intervals along the heading, through the bottom set of slots. The manufacturer or stockist will have recommended a certain number of hooks per metre. The standard recommendation is one every 7 or 8 cm. If you have made a short unlined curtain in a lightweight fabric you may use fewer. A floor-length curtain in velvet, lined and interlined, would need the maximum support to prevent the

3 Lay the curtain out wrong side up. Pass the long point of the hook up through the slot in the heading, then turn it towards you. There should be a hook every 7 or 8 cm.

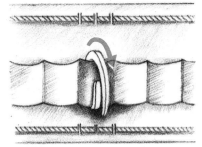

heading bowing away from the track.

Lay the curtain out wrong side up, and hold the hook with the long point away from you facing towards the top of the curtain. Pass the long point up through the back of the slot in the heading, then turn it towards you (see fig 3). The curled eyes will stop it going right through the curtain, and the long point will now be downwards, ready to hook into the glider.

Insert the hooks all the way along the heading at your chosen intervals. Make sure you have hooks at the ends or as near to the ends as possible, but don't put a hook through the hole

where the coiled cord emerges. Put a hook outside that cord if there is a space available.

If the track has a 'return' – in other words bends round a short distance at each side to fit the curve of a recess – put a hook in at the very end of each curtain with the next at the corner. Don't gather up or pleat the curtain between those points. Likewise, gather up or pleat the curtain less where it will overlap with the other curtain when drawn (fig 4).

If you have left the hem till last, probably because the fabric is heavy, let the curtain hang for a few days with hems unsewn. Then you can take up the hem as though the window were a person and you were taking up a skirt. This will ensure that the bottom edge is level. You could hand-sew the hem with the curtain still hanging which will make the job less cumbersome and

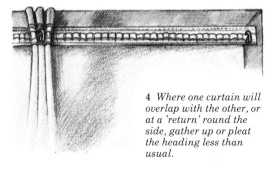

4 Where one curtain will overlap with the other, or at a 'return' round the side, gather up or pleat the heading less than usual.

heavy. Mitre the bottom corners if you leave taking the hem up till last.

You should now press the curtain. If it is long, place two chairs on the other side of the ironing board ready to receive each section as you iron.

Hanging the curtains

Once you have made a pair of curtains, it is essential to hang them well to achieve a good 'set'. If the curtains are long, get someone to stand by the window bearing the weight of the material while you stand on a chair or stepladder

Making linings

It is best to make linings for all curtains except the most informal ones. Lining fabric is a tightly woven cotton, generally in a neutral colour such as cream or white. It is also available in other colours so you can choose one to suit your particular curtain. Beige generally looks acceptable with most colours at the red end of the spectrum (yellows, browns, reds). White tends to go better with blue-green fabrics, and should be used for thin materials with a white background as coloured or beige could show through.

Linings may be permanently or temporarily attached to the curtain, or made separately on their own heading tape and attached to the same hooks as the curtain. The latter method is the most convenient, as the linings can be separated from the curtains when either lining or curtain is due for washing or cleaning. If the two are permanently attached, washing may be cumbersome even if the curtain fabric lends itself to washing. But joining the lining to the curtain will give a better finished appearance.

Standard lining heading tape is manufactured in a 'V' shape with the two sides forming a kind of skirt. One side is slightly wider than the other, and the cord runs along the shorter side. The top edge of the lining fabric lies snugly between the two sides of the skirt (fig 2). The same hooks which carry the curtain will carry the lining. As with the curtains themselves, you will have to make a left-sided and a right-sided lining.

1 All hooks go through the gliders from the front except those at the side edges. Curl the hems round so that the hooks there can be inserted from the rear. The curtain will hang better, and the bundle of cords will be hidden by the fold.

to slot the hooks through the gliders. Fit as many gliders to the track as you have hooks (consult the manufacturer's recommendation). With the hooks in place in the curtain tape, start at either end and slip the hooks into the rings. All hooks go on from the front, except those at the side edges of each curtain. Curl the side hems round and insert these outer two from the rear. It will help to give a good roll to the edge of the curtain, and prevent the hems (and lining if there is one) as well as the cord-tidy or bundle of cord showing from inside the room (fig 1).

Finally ease the gathers or pleating into place. Take a handful of the bottom hem corresponding with the material at the top, and run your cupped hand down the first fold from top to bottom. (Again you will need someone to help you on long curtains.) Push that gather or pleat across to the side and work on subsequent folds all along. To achieve an even folding, tie a piece of tape or strip of fabric round the drawn-back curtain and leave it overnight. (Do not pull too tightly on velvet or you may leave a mark.) The curtain will subsequently fall in the same folds.

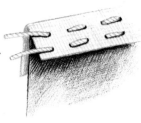

2 Lining heading tape is V-shaped. The top edge of the lining fabric is sewn up into the V with the right side of the lining facing the same direction as the corded side of the tape.

First the measurements. Curtain lining usually comes in 120 cm widths. This may be the same as your curtain fabric width, but if the latter is wider you will have to join widths of lining together.

To determine the length and therefore the amount to buy, refer to the hook drop of your curtain. Deduct 1.5 cm for clearance at the bottom, because the lining will be shorter than the curtain. Add 12 cm for a double 6 cm hem at the bottom and 1.5 cm at the top for attaching the lining fabric to the lining tape. You could reasonably cancel out these figures and regard the total length needed as the curtain hook drop. Then add 10 cm for possibly poor cutting in the shop. Double that figure for making two curtains, and finally round it up to the nearest quarter or half-metre that you are able to buy. Of course you will have to amend the calculation appropriately if you need to join widths (see page 13). You can minimise waste by doing a calculation for several curtains at a time and buying one length which you can cut from as you need the fabric.

Lay out the lining on your table or floor and cut it square at the bottom. Do not use the pulled-thread method as the lining will probably have a slightly moveable grain. Measure and cut as many lengths as you need. For any joins make ordinary flat seams – press them open but do not bother to neaten them.

Turn up the bottom hem by 12 cm and press it flat, then turn in the last 6 cm, and press that too to give you a double 6 cm hem, as on the curtain itself. You can machine-sew along the top of this hem. Turn in and machine-sew double hems down the sides too, the first fold being 4 cm, the second 1.5 cm (see Making up the curtains). You could mitre the corners for a neat finish.

Remembering that you need to make a left-handed and a right-handed version, position the fabric and the lining tape on your sewing machine, with the lining to the left and the tape

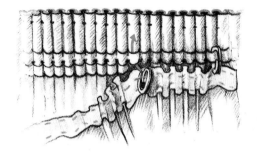

3 *For detachable linings the hooks go up behind the top cord of the lining tape, then up behind the* *bottom cord of the main heading tape before being turned over to slot through the gliders.*

to the right. Feed the lining fabric into the tape, right to the top of the divide, and sew along the top, feeding and sewing as you go. If you find that difficult, start by pinning the fabric into place in the lining tape, then remove the pins as you sew. The shorter, corded, side of the tape should be on the right side of the lining (fig 2).

At the ends, treat the cord exactly as you treated the cord on the main part of the curtain. Unpick the cord to clear the ends. At the inner sides of the lining, pull the cords through on the underside of the tape, knot them, fold the ends under, and sew them down to secure and conceal the knotted ends permanently.

At the outer ends of the tape, pull the cord through on the exposed side of the tape. Knot it temporarily, fold the tape under, and sew it down securely in place. Now pull through the cord to gather up the lining to just less than the finished width of the curtain itself. Form a tidy roll in the excess part of the cord, as on the main heading.

To fit the lining, lay it out on top of the curtain so that the top cord in the lining tape coincides with the bottom cord in the heading tape. Fit the curtain hooks, but slot the hooks through both of these cords (fig 3). The lining will then hang well, with the side hems together.

Fixed lining

One problem with a lining which is made up on a separate lining tape and hung on the same hooks as the curtain is that it tends to hang untidily. This is a special problem with large curtains because of the weight of the lining fabric. The lining droops between the hooks and the curtain tends to hang out of true at the bottom.

You can avoid this by sewing the lining to the curtain. Make up the linings in the same way as in the previous method up to the point where you deal with the top edge. In this system it will have no separate tape. Instead, turn down the top edge to give a 3 cm hem. Lay this top hem so that it just overlaps the bottom of the heading tape on the curtain, and machine-sew the two together. The sewing line should be the same as that which joins the bottom edge of the heading tape to the curtain (fig 1).

The curtain and lining hang as though they were separate, but there is no chance of them gaping apart at the top. When you want to wash or clean the curtains, it is easy to unpick the line of sewing, wash the linings separately (which will save money if you have the curtains themselves dry-cleaned), and sew them together again when they are ready for re-hanging.

Bagged curtain

A third type of construction is the bagged curtain. It entails sewing the linings to the curtains round three sides. It has the advantage of simplicity, and you may find it useful for fairly small curtains.

Measure up and join widths as in the basic curtain process, for both the curtain and lining. Cut the curtain fabric following the formula given on page 12. Cut the lining to the length and width of what will be the finished flat curtain – i.e. the curtain's hook drop plus the heading height above the hook.

Lay the lining on the curtain, right sides together, placing the top edge of the lining 7.5 cm below the top edge of the curtain. Notch the selvedges and then sew the sides together 1.5 cm in from the edges, beginning at the top of the lining and finishing about 20 cm from the bottom.

Turn up a double 2.5 cm hem on the bottom of the lining, and machine-sew it. Turn up a double 7.5 cm hem on the curtain fabric and hand-sew it, mitring the corners. Turn the whole assembly inside out, and adjust the fabrics to give equal side hems to the curtain fabric. Pin and press them in place. Hand-sew the lining to the curtain as far as the bottom (fig 2).

At the top, turn the curtain fabric down over the lining to give the correct curtain length. Mitre the corners and sew on the heading tape. The top edge of the lining can be left raw because it will be covered by the heading tape.

1 *If you want to sew the lining to the curtain, the stitching through the top of the hem of the lining should line up with the bottom stitching on the curtain heading tape.*

2 *For bagged curtains, take up the hems of the lining and the curtain separately. Then hand-sew the bottoms of the seams which you have so far left free to give room for manoeuvre.*

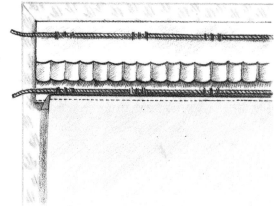

Locked-in lining

The professional way to line curtains is to lock them in. It is worth the extra trouble as it will greatly improve the hang of the curtains. The lining should be 8 cm narrower and 4 cm shorter than the finished flat curtain. Join widths and press the seams open. Press in a single 6 cm hem down each side of the curtain, and a single 15 cm bottom hem, with mitred corners. Secure the hems with a loose slipstitch.

Lay the curtain out on your flat surface, right side facing downwards. With the help of a metre rule and dressmaker's chalk (or pins for a loose-woven, fabric) draw vertical lines down the curtain at intervals of about 30 cm. The intervals can be greater on a very wide curtain.

Then lay the lining on top of the curtains, wrong side to wrong side. Fold back one edge of the lining until you can see the first chalk or pin line. Starting about 18 cm from the top of the curtain, lockstitch the two pieces of fabric together, making large stitches about 10 cm apart. Don't pull the thread tight and only pick up one or two threads each time – otherwise the stitching will show on the right side of the curtain (fig 3). Continue until you get to the hem line of the curtain. Repeat across the curtain.

When you have locked the lining to the curtain across its entire width, turn and press the lining fabric 2 cm in at the sides, and 4 cm at the bottom. Slipstitch the lining to the curtain hem all round to close the hems.

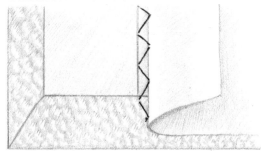

3 *When lockstitching the lining to the curtain make large stitches and pick up only a couple of threads at each stitch – otherwise the stitches will show on the front of the curtain.*

Interlining

Curtains generally look perfectly acceptable if they are made with good lining. But there is a further step that gives them an appearance of extra luxury, with a roll at the edges and fullness of folding normally expected on only the most expensive products. It consists of a third layer of fabric fitted between the curtains and the lining.

Interlining is not merely decorative, but it also provides considerable additional insulation. It is generally made of rough and soft flannel called bump or domette, which stops the passage of air and so keeps the heated air inside a warm room, by preventing heat being conducted from the warm room to the cold area behind the curtain.

There is also available a metallic fabric called milium designed specifically as a heat insulator. You can use this as a lining – but interlining may still be necessary to improve the look of the curtains. But ordinary bump or domette fitted as interlining works extremely well.

Cut the interlining to the same dimensions as the main fabric. You may need to join widths, in which case use a run-and-fell seam as interlining tends to stretch.

Deal with the interlining before you tackle the lining. On your large surface, spread out the unsewn curtain right side down with the interlining on top of it, matching the bottom and side edges. Fold the interlining in half and lockstitch it to the curtain down the fold line. Make other rows of lockstitching across the curtain at intervals of about 30 cm, depending on the width of the fabric.

Then fold in about 5 cm at the bottom and each side, treating the curtain fabric and interlining as one. Mitre the corners – you could trim away the interlining here so that the corner is less bulky. Slipstitch the hems and corners in place.

Now lay the lining on top of the interlined curtain and continue as if you were merely lining a curtain.

Pelmets and valances

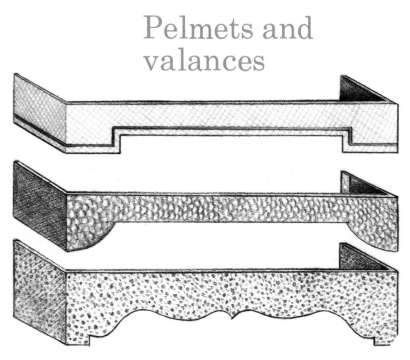

1 *A range of pelmet designs. No point along the front of the pelmet should hang lower than the 'returns' at the sides, which should have a straight bottom edge.*

Window dressings go in and out of fashion with remarkable regularity. There was a time recently when pelmets were considered too fussy to bother with, and everybody seemed to prefer the uncluttered lines of a simple decorative heading. Inevitably, the fashion swung back, and pelmets and valances have a certain popularity once more.

The pelmet is especially suitable for large windows in Georgian or Victorian houses, and it is an excellent design device for linking two windows. It can also disguise poorly proportioned windows if it is mounted higher or lower than the window or extended beyond it at the sides.

Basically, the pelmet is a shaped piece of buckram covered with fabric and mounted on to a shelf, concealing the curtain track. It can be straight-edged or shaped. Usually it is made out of the same fabric as the one used to make the curtains or blind, but it is possible to achieve dramatic effects with a contrasting fabric. You can achieve a softer line by fitting interlining material between the buckram and the fabric. A good pelmet starts with the design – fig 1 shows a range of possibilities. The choice runs from a straight, unfussy version, through a variety of more or less simple curves, to the elaborate kind of design shown last.

For a softer line you could consider making a frilled valance – they are similar to pelmets and perform much the same function in concealing the curtain track while giving a good design finish to the window. They may be lined but are often left unlined to take advantage of their frilly and billowing appearance. They are especially suitable on cottage and bedroom windows, particularly in an informal patterned print or chintz.

A valance is far simpler to make than a pelmet. It can be nailed to a board, just as a pelmet is, or fitted to a track separate from the curtains with its own hooks and rings.

Practise drawing a few alternatives until you arrive at a pelmet or valance which you feel suits your window but which hides the curtain track properly.

Making the pelmet board

First fit your pelmet board – this is really just like putting up a shelf. You need a piece of wood, probably hardboard or plywood, 10–15 cm wide, 15–20 mm thick, and long enough to cover the window and just clear the curtains at the end (5 cm would be enough unless you want to alter the window's proportions).

Pelmets are sometimes given vertical wooden 'returns' which make the structure into a sort of box, but a simple shelf is perfectly adequate if your carpentry isn't up to that. If you are fitting a pelmet into a recess you won't need returns. If

2 *Join widths of fabric with one complete width in the centre. Match up the pattern with smaller sections to either side.*

3 *Turn the template over to get a mirror image for the other half of the buckram. Mark the centre point and the start of the returns.*

you are fitting a pelmet round a bay, you will have to shape and plane the wood to follow the curve, which requires higher woodworking skills, or you will have to buy the pelmet board ready-made.

Fix enough brackets to the wall with enough screws to bear the weight of the board itself, plus the curtains, plus any stress that will occur when the curtains are drawn.

The track should be fixed to the underside of the pelmet board. Almost all types of track have fittings which can be screwed on horizontally or vertically. The vertical arrangement suits the pelmet. One advantage of the pelmet system over plain tracks is that you can arrange the tracks in two straight parts, with one overlapping the other by a substantial amount. Fit the two parts of the track to overlap by about 15 cm: this gives a better line than the alternative of bending one of the tracks. It is also possible to buy fittings which hold the edge of the curtain out to produce an overlap. They are a perfectly good choice and you need then only fit one continuous length of track. Try the board in place for measurement. Then take it down to fit the pelmet fabric to it.

Making up the pelmet

To make the pelmet itself, you will need a length of buckram. Buy the best you can afford for the best finish. To establish its length, measure along the pelmet board and add the lengths of the two returns (the pelmet will have returns even if the board doesn't). Its depth will be the greatest depth on your design – normally this will be the same depth as the returns. It is not good design to have any point on the front of the pelmet hanging lower than the returns, and the returns themselves should be straight, front-to-back. Make a template from brown paper of half your finished design, from one side to the centre. Try it at the window before laying it on the buckram. Remember to add the length of the return at the end. With dressmaker's chalk and on both sides of the buckram, draw round the design, turn the template over on its end, and repeat the process for the other side. Mark clearly the centre and the points where the returns start (fig 3). If you need to join lengths of buckram, butt them together and apply another short length of buckram as backing. Moist heat will soften the glue impregnating the buckram, so dampen the contact surfaces with a sponge and go over the area with a hot iron, covering the buckram with brown paper first to prevent glue getting on to the iron. Cut out the buckram.

Then turn to the fabric. If the pelmet needs more than one width, as most do, fit a complete width in the centre. For the fabric at the sides cut a width in half and fit half of it on each side of the complete centrally placed width (fig 2). Match the patterns to join the sections, and sew the

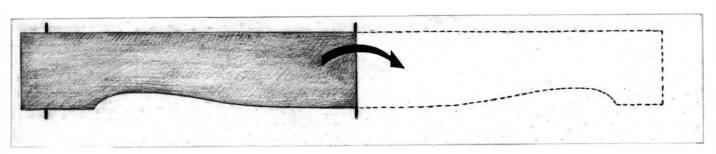

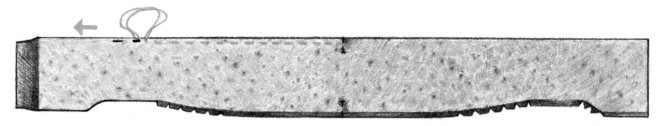

1 *Tack the fabric to the buckram. Using doubled cotton, start at the centre top and work outwards. Turn the raw edge of the fabric over to the back of the buckram and sew through all three layers, stretching the fabric as you go. When you get to the edge start again at the centre and work outwards in the opposite direction.*

For the bottom edge, snip into the fabric to enable it to go round the curves and into the corners. Tack it in the same way as the top edge.

seams right sides together. Press the seams open.

Lay the buckram on the fabric, and cut round it, leaving a 2.5 cm margin of fabric for working, and 2.5 cm at each end in addition to the length of the returns. The buckram will probably tend to curve, however long you leave it unrolled. Use the concave side of the curve as the front of the pelmet: that will eventually give a better 'set' to the finished job, particularly at the corners.

If you plan to use interlining to help soften the appearance, fit it at this stage. Lay bump or domette over the front of the buckram, butting any joins to make up the full width, and trim it to the exact shape and size of the buckram. Go over it with a warm iron (again, protect the iron with brown paper) and the melted glue will set to fix the bump in place. Check that it is accurately trimmed.

With your covering fabric seamed, cut out and the selvedge removed, locate the centre and mark it with pins at the top and bottom. If the fabric is plain, fold it in two to find the centre; the centre may be clear on some fabrics.

Lay the fabric on the buckram, and pin the two firmly together at the exact centre, top and bottom. The task now is to smooth the fabric out over the buckram, without pulling it off centre, without distorting the fabric, and without putting wrinkles into it.

The best way to do this is by sewing as it gives a softer line. Using doubled cotton and starting at the centre top, turn the margin of the fabric over evenly to the back of the buckram, and sew with a tacking stitch right along the top of the pelmet, towards the left. Stretch the fabric

outwards as you go, to give a good taut finish. When you get to the left end, secure and break the thread, go back to the centre and sew outwards to the right side (fig 1).

For the bottom edge, snip the fabric to go round all the convex curves, and cut small wedges into the corners (fig 1). The skilful part is to pull and cut the fabric to the correct point for taking out all the tension and rucking, while at the same time not cutting so far that the buckram shows and the fabric frays. Tack it with the same stitch as the straight top edge. Trim the vertical ends of the fabric to about 1.5 cm and turn them in.

Fixing the pelmet

What you do next depends on whether you plan to fix the pelmet permanently or make it detachable for dry-cleaning. If it is to be a permanent fixture there are two alternatives. You can line it first (see below), fix it to the board along the top and sides with metal tacks, and then glue on the braid to cover the tacks (fig 2). This will need an accurate eye while you are up a stepladder. Or you can sew on the braid or fringe, and line the pelmet so that the stitching is concealed. Then apply a length of curtain heading tape of a matching colour (turning under the raw ends) by sewing down the tape at intervals of about 10 cm, making sure that the stitching does not go through to the front fabric (fig 3). You can then push a drawing-pin through the heading tape into the edge of the board at the centre of each 'pocket'.

2 & 3 *Permanent methods of fixing a pelmet to the board. Hammer in tacks along the top and sides and then cover the tacks with glued-on braid; or sew heading tape invisibly to the back of the fabric at 10 cm intervals – you can then push a drawing-pin through the centre of each 'pocket' in the tape.*

4 & 5 *Methods of fixing a pelmet if you want to be able to remove it. Sew on rings at each end and hammer corresponding nails into the returns; or glue Velcro strips to the ends of the pelmet and the board.*

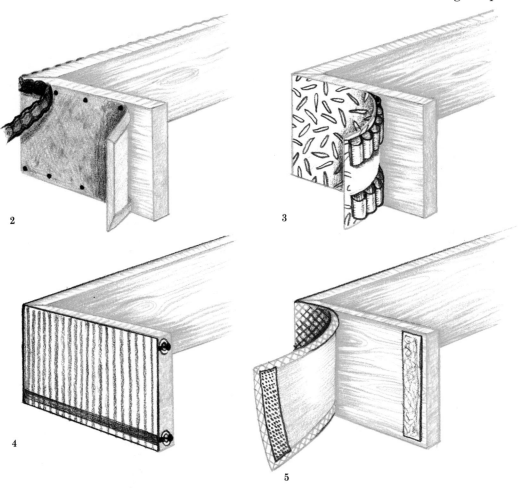

2

3

4

5

The alternatives if you want the pelmet to be removable for cleaning are to trim and line it, then sew on small brass or plastic rings at each end, and hammer nails into the edges of the returns to correspond (fig 4). The fit must be very taut or the pelmet will sag where it has no attachment along the front.

Otherwise glue a strip of Velcro to each side of the board and sew on the corresponding strip to the return of the pelmet (fig 5). Do this after applying the trimming and lining. Again, the fit must be very exact.

At whichever stage you apply the lining, you need to cut lining fabric to the same shape as the pelmet but add on seam allowances of 1 cm all round. Pin it centrally in position, then gradually slipstitch round, snipping into the allowance to ease any curves. Neither stitching nor lining fabric should be visible from the front. Attach the pelmet by your chosen method.

Valances

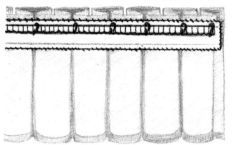 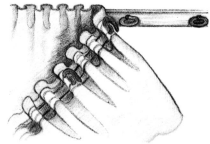 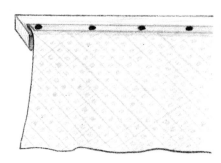

1 *For a washable valance, draw it up to the length you want and insert enough hooks to fit the rail.*

2 *Or place the curtain hooks through small eye hooks screwed along the front of the board.*

3 *A valance can be permanently fixed by enclosing the top edge within bias binding, and then hammering in tacks through the binding.*

A simple valance is a length of fabric gathered into a series of frills, or more formally drawn up into a series of triple or pinch pleats. The depth of the valance depends on the size and proportions of the window and curtains; generally it is between one-sixth and one-ninth of the height from curtain rail to floor (25 cm approximately). Add 12 cm for a 3–5 cm heading and the hem at the bottom. Cut and sew widths of fabric to make up the valance width. The fabric used should be not less than 1½ times the distance across the front of the curtains, plus the returns. Thin flimsy fabrics may need more than this, while heavier fabrics will hang awkwardly if too much is used.

Making up the valance for fitting to a rail is nearly the same as making up a curtain. Turn down the top hem, and sew on a simple heading tape as on page 15. Check the height of the valance, and turn up a small double hem at the bottom to the height you want. Draw up the valance to the appropriate length, and insert hooks to fit the curtain rail, including fixed ones at each end (fig 1).

An alternative type of valance has a pencil pleated heading. Use one of the special types of tape with its correct hooks. The valance can be fixed on to a valance rail or a pelmet board. If you are fitting it to a board, screw small eye hooks along the front edge of the board at intervals that correspond with the hooks in the tape (fig 2).

The other way to deal with the valance is to enclose the top raw edge in bias binding, stitching close to the edges, and then hammering tacks through the binding all along the board (fig 3).

If the fabric is not sufficiently firm, apply a stiffener to prevent the heading from sagging. Make up a length of interfacing, deep enough to fit from the top of the finished valance to the bottom of the heading tape – this will provide the necessary 'body'. Lockstitch it into place as described on page 21, and finally sew it when you sew on the heading tape.

Some fabrics are so soft that it is worth lining the valance as well as stiffening the heading with interfacing. If you are using all the choices – fabric, interfacing, interlining and lining – cut the interfacing and interlining to the finished length and depth of the valance. First fit the interfacing in place, then the interlining. Lockstitch the interlining to the interfacing at intervals of about 30 cm. Lockstitch the lining to the interlining at similar intervals.

Turn in the allowances of the lining and fabric, and slipstitch along the top, bottom and ends. Then sew on the heading tape following the directions on page 15.

You will have to experiment to see whether the full range of layers is suitable for your fabric and design. If it makes it too stiff, omit either the interfacing, or the interlining.

Swags and tails

4 *A typical swag has this shape before it is pleated up into its folds. The deeper the curve the deeper will be the finished swag. Transfer the pleating points from the pattern along the two sides.*

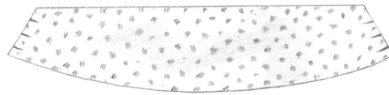

5 *Starting from the top, pin each pleat in place before trying the swag in position.*

These are an elaborate extension of the pelmet or valance, and are appropriate on tall windows only. They are sometimes called draperies or draped pelmets. The style was popular in Victorian and Edwardian residences, and the most suitable fabrics are correspondingly luxurious – satin, velvet and taffeta, for instance. Modern synthetic fabrics such as Dupion would also be possible. Avoid stiff fabrics as they don't hang well. The style can be successfully brought up to date with some of the newer loose-weave fabrics in muted beiges and browns. The swags and tails will probably be in the same fabric as the curtains.

They use an appreciable amount of material so do your sums before embarking on a scheme which calls for their extensive use. It would be advisable to have a rehearsal first with lengths of muslin or an old but well-ironed sheet.

Swags

The swag – the part that hangs in folds across the top of the curtains – is fixed to the same kind of board as a pelmet, so carry out the woodwork and attach the curtain track to it before you start.

Then consider the proportions of the swag. The taller the window the deeper the swag. On a narrow window, a single swag may be all that is needed. A wide window may be able to carry a set of three or perhaps even five, overlapping so that alternate ones emerge from behind the others. If you make them overlap, make sure they do so at a good clear angle – the effect of the swags will be lost if they appear to merge into one continuous run.

The two important factors to get right are the angle of the sides of the pattern from the vertical, and the shape of the curved bottom edge. If the angle is acute, and the curve pronounced, the folds of the finished swag will be deep. If the angle and the curve are shallow, the finishing folds on the swag will also be shallow. You will find out what is best for your window when experimenting with the muslin.

You will need to measure and mark the points down the sides of the swag at which the folds will occur. Folding points at intervals of 15–18 cm are right for most purposes. The best effect is achieved by a small number of pronounced folds rather than several skimpy ones.

When you have outlined the pattern, cut out the fabric. Cut half of the pattern, then double the fabric along its length and cut the other half to achieve a neat symmetrical curve; or fold the fabric parallel to the selvedges before you cut.

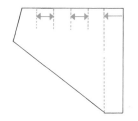

1

2

3

The approximate shape of the swag's pattern will be as in fig 4 on page 27. Cut an identical piece of lining fabric, and sew it to the main fabric right sides together down the two sides and along the bottom. Trim the corners, neaten the seams, and then turn the fabrics right side out.

Transfer the planned pleating points from the pattern along the two sides. Starting from the top, pin each pleat in place (fig 5 on page 27). Try the swag in position. Then sew the pleats firmly into place, and attach the swag to the board along the top edge by hammering in tacks, having turned under the top raw edge.

Tails

Tails invariably accompany swags to break the line at the edge of the window; they are sometimes incorporated along the window to trim the junctions between swags.

They may be in the same fabric as the swags and the curtains but you could use contrasting fabrics. Tails should be lined on the reverse side because parts will show from the front. The lining could be the same or a contrasting fabric.

The pattern for a tail is shown in fig 1. There will be one at each side of the curtain so cut reverse pairs. This type of tail is not normally used between swags (see below). You may choose between a straight line along the bottom edge, or a convex or concave curve. A concave curve will reveal more of the reverse side of the fabric. The angle of the bottom will alter the set of the swags. Experiment with bits of muslin to see the effects produced by the various patterns.

Make five marks at equal intervals along the top of the edge of the pattern to divide it into six sections. Fold the sections mark-to-mark, as shown in fig 2. When you have seen the effect and determined your pattern, cut the matching pair from your finished fabric. Sew fabric to lining right sides together round the sides and bottom edge. Trim the corners of the seam to avoid bulkiness and turn the tail right side out. Fold it into the pleats you decided on. Sew the top edge to the finished shape, and fit it to the swag board by turning under the top raw edge and hammering in a couple of tacks. Complete the tail for the other side of the window.

Pleated centre tails

The traditional means of trimming the curtain between the swags includes several versions of a short centre tail, cut symmetrically.

A plain pleated centre tail is shown in fig 3. Ideally, the lowest point should be no longer than the shortest pleat on the outside tails. Cut and line the fabric, turn it inside out, and fold it into pleats as indicated by the marks.

All swags and tails can be finished by sewing them into a contrasting band of fabric, double-folded to form two double hems so that all the raw edges are enclosed within it (fig 4). The band can then be turned over the top of the swag fixing board, and tacked or pinned in place. You could also attach tassels or cord as further embellishments.

4

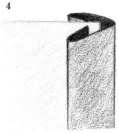

1 & 2 Cut two side tails in reverse of each other. Divide each tail into six and fold up the sections.

3 A pleated centre tail hangs symmetrically and is shorter than a side tail.

4 The tops of swags and tails are enclosed in a double folded band.

Net curtains

Net curtains are most commonly used for maintaining privacy and hiding an ugly view while letting in the light. In some circumstances you could consider using café curtains (page 33) or a blind (page 37) instead.

A variety of manufactured heading tapes are now made specifically for use with nets. You will need a rail with hooks and rings for fitting the net, so that method is probably more suited to larger windows where the heading will be high enough to be obscured. Fit whichever heading tape you choose as if you were making ordinary curtains (see page 15).

For smaller windows, the old-fashioned method of sewing a casing into the net for slotting through a plastic-coated wire is simple and unobtrusive, and calls for a minimum of sewing. Nets normally hang within the window recess. Cut the wire to give just enough tension so that it holds taut. Insert two tiny cuphooks into the window frame at the sides and two tiny eyes into the ends of the wire rod. Fit the wire 2.5 cm down from the top of the available space for the net to allow room for the heading (fig 5).

Measure the length of the curtain from the wire to the window sill, or to the bottom of the frame, according to your preference and the type of window. The width of the curtain should be up to $1\frac{1}{2}$ times the width of the window – more will make the net too bunched up round the casing.

Allow a total of 6 cm for two doubled 1.5 cm side hems. To the finished length of fabric, add 7.5 cm at the top for the casing and heading, and 15 cm at the bottom for a double 7.5 cm hem.

It is possible to join widths of net if you need to although many nets are sold wide enough to avoid the necessity. Because the net is translucent any joins will show slightly. Join widths with either a French or a run-and-fell seam – the seam must of course be on the wrong side of the fabric. Use a fine no 9 sewing-machine needle and a fairly large stitch. It helps to insert layers of tissue paper between the layers of net to stop everything slipping around while you are sewing.

Sew the two side hems first, each a doubled 1.5 cm. Then turn up and sew the bottom double 7.5 cm hem. If you want to weight the hem add the weights at this stage – the string-of-sausages type are the best ones for net curtains. At the top, turn down the fabric at the 7.5 cm mark, and fold under the first 2.5 cm. Sew the fold down to the fabric, then sew along the line just below the raw edge, to produce a heading of 2.5 cm, and a casing of about 2.5 cm (fig 6). Thread the net on to the wire, ease out the folds, and hook up the wire.

5 When hanging net curtains, fit the wire 2.5 cm down from the top of the space to allow room for the heading.

6 Make a casing for the wire by sewing two lines of stitching about 2.5 cm apart through the folded hem. The wire is fixed to the frame by tiny screw eyes and cuphooks.

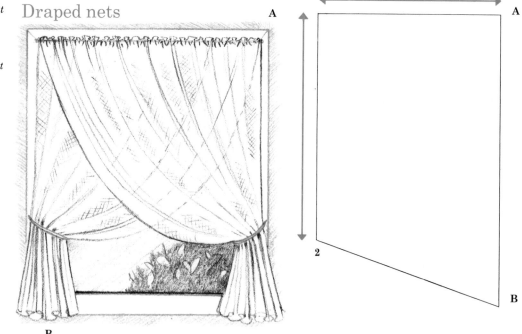

1 *Draped nets let in light but help to maintain privacy, especially on large windows.*

2 *The sort of shape to cut the net. The longer side (**AB**) will be the inner edge of the curtain.*

A traditional design for nets, intended to set off the curtains as much as to stop people peering in, is the type of net draped to the sides of the window (fig 1). They are especially effective on large and full-length windows.

If necessary, join widths to give adequate fullness, using a narrow French or run-and-fell seam. To determine the number of widths to use, divide the window width into three. Each curtain occupies two thirds of that width, so that they overlap across the middle third of the window. Use 2–2½ times the finished width in each curtain. (The curtains could overlap completely for even greater privacy.)

The length is slightly complicated because of the effect of the drape. The fabric must be cut to accommodate the additional length, so the pattern for cutting will be longer on one side than on the other. Fig 2 shows the effect. To calculate what those lengths should be, pin a piece of string to the window frame at the point **A** where a curtain will start, drape it loosely to the point where the tie-back will hold it, and let it hang to the sill or floor, depending on where the bottom hem of the curtain will fall (**B**). The other side is a straight measurement.

Add 7.5 cm for the heading and casing, and 2.5 cm for a double hem at the bottom. Make two curtains in reverse of each other for opposite sides. Because of the overlap, you will need two plastic-coated wires to hang the curtains on but you can fit them on to the same hooks at the sides of the window frame.

The curtains will need tie-backs to hold them in the draped position. Cut a piece of plain net 10 cm wide and 30 cm long. Turn in the ends by 1.5 cm and fold the sides to the centre. This will give a strip 2.5 cm wide and 27 cm long. Close the ends and open side by slipstitching, and sew a small ring to each end for fitting over a hook.

Nets with a frilled hem

Festoon nets

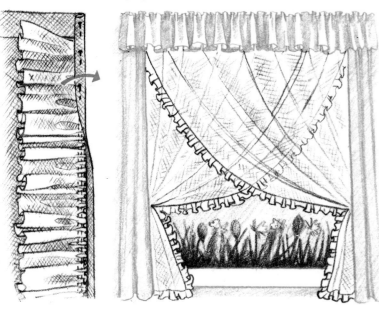

3 & 4 Attach a frill to a net curtain by drawing it up on its gathering threads. Lay the frill a centimetre in from the curtain's edge, right sides together, and sew the seam. Turn the longer seam allowance over the frill's raw edge in order to neaten it.

Many nets come with the frill already attached, but to make one, cut four long strips of net each 12 cm wide, and the length of the inner side hem.

Join two of the strips together and fold the resulting strip lengthwise to enclose the short seam. Then fold in the two long edges and make two rows of gathers along that edge.

Give the curtains a double 1.5 cm hem along the bottom and up the outside edges. Press down the top hem to form the 2.5 cm casing and the 2.5 cm heading, or attach heading tapes.

The inside edge of the curtain is the important one. Draw the frill up on its gathering threads to this length. Lay the frill parallel to the curtain, about a centimetre in from the edge and starting it 2.5 cm from the top so that it doesn't get in the way of the casing (fig 3). Sew the two together, right sides together, then turn the longer seam allowance of the curtain over the frill's raw edges (fig 4). Press down the seam.

The ultimate in elaborate decoration for a window is a set of festoon nets. The billowing curves provide privacy but admit light, and give a softness of line which is perhaps particularly suited to bedrooms. In living-rooms, a large floor-length window may be necessary to do justice to the effect. It is best to look on them as a permanent feature – if you want something similar that can be lowered and raised, Austrian or festoon blinds might be the answer (page 41).

Festoon nets are quite extravagant in fabric. You will need at least 1½ times the width and up to three times the height of the window.

Calculate the dimensions of the festoons. The example illustrated is for a 120 cm wide window. It gives four 30 cm festoons. To make up, festoons require casings, formed on the wrong side of the net, on which to draw up the fabric. The points at which to make these casings should be 30, 60, and 90 cm across the curtain after the fabric is drawn up to the finished width. Take account of the side hems in your calculations. If you need to join widths, make run-and-fell seams that coincide with the casings.

Start by sewing the vertical casings into the length of the netting. Make two lines of stitching about 1.5 cm apart. Cut lengths of piping cord the length of the window. Thread the piping into the casings with a safety pin.

Turn down and sew the top of the net to make the double heading which will be the casing for the wire, sewing across the piping cord as you go. Pin up the bottom hem and sew it in place, again going across the piping to fix it (fig 2 overleaf). Adjust the fabric bunched up by the piping – you may find this easier if you lay the curtain out on the floor so that the festoons will stay where you arrange them. At intervals of 10 or 12 cm down each vertical casing pin the folds to the piping – the pinning points must all be level (fig 1 overleaf). Insert the wire through the top casing, and

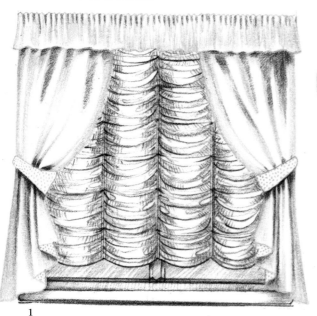

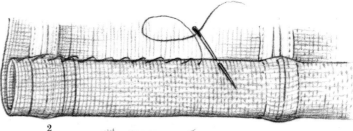

1

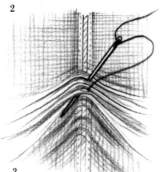

3

1 *The pinning points gathering up the festoons must be level across the curtain.*

2 *Sew the bottom hem by going across the piping.*

3 *Anchor the festoons in place by sewing firmly through each pinning point.*

Tie-backs

try the curtain up against the window to see if the festoons are hanging neatly and equally. When you are satisfied with the hang, take the curtain down and sew through each pinning point to anchor the festoons in place (fig 3).

Sew on any fringes or tassels to the hem or the bottoms of the vertical casings, although you may find the curtain is already sufficiently decorative. Then the curtain is ready to hang properly.

It is possible to buy a narrow lightweight nylon gathering tape, which you can simply sew on to the back of the curtain at the required intervals, then pull up the net to give the festoons.

4 Tie-backs can be as plain or decorative as you want, in keeping with your curtain scheme.

The appearance of many curtains and bed hangings is improved by being held open with a tie-back (fig 4). You can buy tasselled silk rope in many colours which should enable you to match your curtain fabric, but a much cheaper and more individual approach would be to make your own, in either the same fabric as the curtain or in a contrasting one. The tie-back is generally stiffened with interlining such as heavyweight Vilene, or buckram, depending on how firm you want it to be. It could be lined on the reverse if you don't want both sides to be in the same fabric.

4

Hold a fabric tape measure round the open or partially open curtain, depending on your preference, as if the tape measure were the tie-back. If the curtains are floor-length an appropriate position for the tie-back would be approximately level with the bottom of the window. Don't pull the curtain too tightly as it will hang wrongly and even mark the fabric.

Note the length of the measure required and add on 2 cm or so for turnings. At the same time mark in pencil the point on the wall where you want the hook or other attachment to go, and fix it in place.

Cut out two strips of fabric for each tie-back, or one strip each of main fabric and lining material. They should be about 12 cm deep (including seam allowances) and the length already established. If you want rounded or pointed ends, shape the material accordingly.

Cut a piece of interfacing to the finished dimension of the tie-back. Tack it to the back of one strip (to the back of the main fabric if you are having a lining side), and catchstitch it in position.

Pin and tack the other strip to the first strip, right sides together, and then machine-sew all the way round leaving an opening about 10 cm long down one long side. Grade the seams and clip the corners and any curves.

Turn the tie-back right sides out through the gap you left, press it and slipstitch the gap closed.

Sew on a ring by hand at each end to fit on to the hook fixed to the wall.

Café curtains

Café curtains are an attractive and well-established way of dressing a window. They fit over the bottom half of the window which gives privacy to people sitting in the room, traditionally of course diners eating at café tables. At the same time they give a view of the outside world to people standing up, and let in daylight through the top half of the window. In some circumstances you could consider them as an alternative to net curtains.

Café curtains look especially good on sash windows where the frame anyway divides the window into two halves with a horizontal bar. The curtains can be fitted to the height of this bar for a neat visual effect. You could consider hanging café curtains with a matching pelmet.

There are many ways of making café curtains. Most types fit on a rod – brass, wood, or stainless steel. The rod will fit into two end sockets, after the curtain is hung on it, or you can use other arrangements of end fixing. A hardware store

5 *Three methods of hanging café curtains: rings sewn or clipped on to a straight top hem, or sewn on to a scalloped edge. In each case the pole is slotted through the rings.*

1

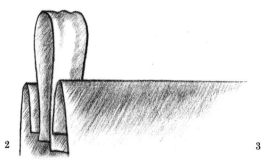

2

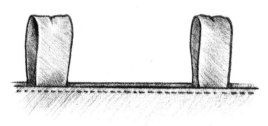

3

1 To make a tab fold each piece right sides together along its length.

2 Press open the seam, turn the tab inside out and position it between the folded down curtain and lining so that its seam is hidden centrally underneath.

3 Stitch along the top edge of the curtain to fix the tabs in place.

should be able to provide you with a good range of rods and fittings.

One of the simplest methods is to attach clip-on rings through which the pole is slotted. You make up the curtain in the usual way, but also turn down the top heading into a double hem, forming mitred corners there too. Then clip on the rings at regular intervals across the top.

Or you can sew large curtain rings along the top edge at intervals of about 10 cm with a neat buttonhole stitch (fig 5 on page 33). Again the top hem should be completed first in the same way as the bottom hem.

A cased heading is the next easiest method and suitable for sheer fabrics – see page 29.

A method more usually associated with café curtains is to sew tabs along the top edge for the pole to go through.

Make up the basic curtain first. The length will be from a point about 7.5 cm below the rod to the bottom point of the finished curtain. Add 15 cm for a double 7.5 cm bottom hem, and 2.5 cm for a top hem. Café curtains should not be too full, so $1\frac{1}{2}$ times the width of the pole is ample. Add 10 cm for a double 2.5 cm hem at each side.

They look best from the outside if they are lined – the bagged type of lining works well (page 20). Make up the curtains except for the top edge.

Make up the tabs from the same fabric as the curtains. Cut enough tabs to fit at 15 cm intervals along the width of the curtain. Measure the circumference of the pole, add on a total of 2.5 cm for seam allowances and another 5 cm or so for room for manoeuvre. This will be the length of the piece of material to cut for each tab. The finished width will be about 6 or 7 cm, so double that for the two sides and add on 2.5 cm for seam allowances to find out the width for cutting.

Fold each piece in two along its length, right sides together, without creasing the fold. Sew along the seam 1.5 cm in from the edge (fig 1). Open out the seam, and press it. Turn the tab inside out, position the seam down the centre of the tab, and press down the side folds. Press the seam allowances of the curtain and its lining in towards each other by 2.5 cm. Pin the tabs 15 cm apart so that all the raw edges are enclosed – allow a 1.25 cm seam allowance at each end of the tab (fig 2).

Try the curtain on the pole to see that all the tabs lie comfortably. Then remove it from the pole and stitch along the top edge of the curtain so that the tabs are fixed in place and the top edge is closed (fig 3).

Scalloped café curtains

Another popular style is one in which the fabric itself is cut in a scalloped pattern and the curtain is hung on the rod with a set of rings.

The curtains are best lined (although see below for how to make facings for the scalloped edge if you don't want to line them). In this case the curtains should be barely wider than the window – otherwise the effect of the scallops will be lost. About $1\frac{1}{4}$ times the width of the curtain would be appropriate. Add on 2.5 cm for the side seams. The total height (which will be cut into to

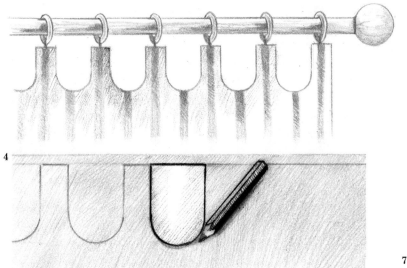

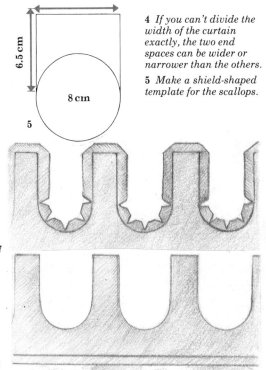

4 *If you can't divide the width of the curtain exactly, the two end spaces can be wider or narrower than the others.*

5 *Make a shield-shaped template for the scallops.*

6 *Mark the positions of the scallops on the lining side of the curtain.*

7 *Sew round the markings and clip the corners and curves.*

8 *If you don't line the curtains, the scallops need to be faced. Give the facing double hems.*

shape the scallops) will be from about 3 cm below the pole to the sill, plus 2.5 cm for turnings.

Join the fabric and lining, right sides together, down the sides. Trim the seams, but don't turn the tube inside out. Pin the top edges together.

Then make a template for the scallops. A generally satisfactory width is about 8 cm with about 3 cm in between each scallop, but the width of the curtain will dictate their exact width and positioning. If it turns out to be tricky dividing the curtain into these measurements, the two end spaces can be increased (fig 4). Draw a circle with the aid of a pair of compasses – the radius should be 4 cm. Draw horizontally across the circle's diameter and from each end draw a line 6.5 cm long at right angles (fig 5).

On the lining side, mark in pencil the position of each scallop according to the scheme you have worked out. Mark a line parallel to the top edge, 1.25 cm in (fig 6). Then sew round the markings as in fig 7. Clip into the curves and cut off the corners so that the scallops will be able to lie flat. Turn the curtain inside out and press it carefully, especially round the scallops. Sew a curtain ring to the centre of each space between the scallops. Turn in the bottom hems to the correct height, slipstitch them together, and press them.

If you don't want to make a lining, cut a piece of material for facing the scallops. It should extend a couple of centimetres below them.

Join the facing to the main fabric down the side seams as before. Then draw in the scallop positions and sew them before giving the bottom of the facing, and the sides and bottom of the fabric, double 2.5 cm hems (fig 8).

Shower curtains

Shower curtains differ from other curtains in several ways – they aren't as full, probably only up to $1\frac{1}{2}$ times as wide as the area to screen; they have a minimum of stitching because the PVC and other waterproof fabrics tear rather easily; they only need single hems because the fabric doesn't fray, and the hooks or loops for fixing them to the shower rail are special for the purpose.

You will need fabric up to $1\frac{1}{2}$ times the width of the area to screen, plus 2.5 cm for each side hem or joined width (allow extra for matching patterns). The length will be from just beneath the shower rail to the floor, plus 2.5 cm for the hem and 4 or 5 cm for the top turning. (You could dispense with side and bottom hems if you wanted.) You will also need a very fine sewing-machine needle, and a special eyelet punch (probably obtainable where you buy the fabric or in a large haberdashery department). Sellotape or paper clips will be a help too. Buy enough hooks (large plastic loop hooks or others recommended by the shop), allowing one for every 15 cm along the top of the curtain.

Join any widths in run-and-fell seams, using a longish length of stitch. If you are making hems, turn in and sew down the sides and along the bottom of the curtain, making single 2.5 cm hems, and mitre the two bottom corners. Turn over the top hem by the amount you allowed (4 or 5 cm) and secure it temporarily with Sellotape or paper clips. During the sewing process, you may find sprinkling a little talcum powder on the fabric will help prevent it sticking.

With the eyelet punch make holes about 15 cm apart along that hem – you don't need to stitch because the bound holes will do the job instead. Peel off the Sellotape or remove the clips. Insert the special hooks and hang the curtain from the shower rail.

1 *Shower curtains need only have single hems with mitred corners. Use Sellotape to hold the fabric temporarily in place while you make the curtain. Fabric widths should be joined in run-and-fell seams. Punch holes along the top hem at intervals of 15 cm.*

Blinds

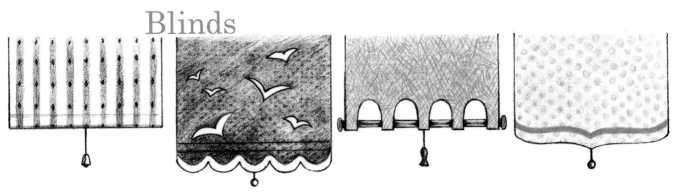

2 *Decorative edgings for the bottoms of roller blinds. The simplest form of decoration is to glue on bobbles or a braid or fringe (the batten may then be several centimetres above the bottom). You could also make a scalloped edge (see café curtains on page 35).*

As an alternative window treatment to curtains, blinds offer several advantages. They need less fabric than curtains. When pulled up they let in more light than a drawn-back curtain so are particularly useful in dark rooms where you need maximum daylight. Furthermore, because they draw up out of the way, they do not obstruct a desk or worktop where a curtain might be inconvenient.

Blinds also have their own decorative purpose. Roller and Roman blinds which leave the fabric flat can show patterned fabrics to advantage in quite a different way from curtains.

Roller blinds

Of the three sorts of blinds described here, roller blinds are probably the most popular. They are uncluttered to look at and easy to clean, especially if made from plastic-coated fabrics, and so are particularly suitable for bathrooms and kitchens. They can be used on their own or in conjunction with curtains, perhaps when privacy is a high priority, and are ideal for dormer windows or ones set into sloping eaves.

You will need a roller blind kit and enough suitable fabric. The kit consists of a wooden roller which the blind winds round; the roller has a square pin at one end which controls the winding mechanism and a round pin at the other.

The round pin comes separate so that you can cut the roller to the exact size required and then hammer the pin into place. Both pins fit into a special bracket fixed to either side of the top of the window. Also in the kit is a wooden batten or lath which is sewn or glued at or near the bottom of the blind for pulling it down; a cord holder and length of cord for fixing to the middle of the batten; and a cord pull with an acorn or other-shaped handle for pulling the blind up or down.

The best fabric for the purpose is holland which comes in a readily usable form since it is stiff enough, does not fray or fade, and can be sponged. It also comes in wide widths which will avoid the need for joins. PVC comes in some bright designs and colours particularly suitable for kitchens and bathrooms where condensation may be a problem.

Other fabrics can be used but must be stiffened, either by dipping them into a special liquid sold alongside the roller blind kits, or by painting or spraying them on both sides. Try to choose a fabric that is wide enough. If the material is plain it might be possible to use it sideways. Joins can be made (by overlapping the edges by about 1 cm once you have stiffened the fabric, being careful to match any pattern, and then gluing the edges together) but are rather obvious when light comes through the blind. You should also test the fabric to see how it responds to dipping, painting or spraying before buying enough to make the blind. In any case you should stiffen the fabric *before* cutting it out since many materials shrink slightly in the process.

It is also possible to buy iron-on or self-adhesive stiffening backings. These are only suitable for small blinds as the added bulk might jam the winding mechanism on a larger blind. Iron or press the backing on to the wrong side of the fabric, starting at the centre so that you can smooth out any wrinkles.

The first step is to measure the window to find out how much material and which size kit to buy. Use a metal or wooden rule – a flexible fabric tape allows too much room for error. Measure the width of window, deciding whether you want the blind to fit within it or extend a little on either side. If it is to go beyond the recess, allow at least 2.5 cm at each side so that direct light is prevented from coming in.

To the length of the window add 30 cm to allow for the batten casing and for the roller to be covered when the shade is pulled right down. If the blind is to be fitted outside the recess, add on another 5 cm at the top so that direct light cannot come in above the window.

The kit to buy is the one where the roller is exactly the width you want or, more likely, the next size up – the roller can be sawn off to the correct length.

Buy material to the total length of the blind (doubled if you are having to join widths) but allow a good 20 cm extra to both dimensions if you are using anything other than holland or PVC, to allow for shrinkage in the course of stiffening. You do not need to take into account any side hems because stiffened fabric does not fray.

Stiffen the fabric if necessary before cutting or joining. When cutting, use the batten as a guideline for marking the fabric and take care to cut all the corners to an exact 90°, using a set square or other reliably right-angled piece of equipment. Examine the fabric to see that any motifs are centrally placed and that any obvious pattern repeat will fall evenly from side to side and also neatly at the bottom of the blind when it is unfurled. If the fabric has to be joined it is better to have a seam at either side to balance the general appearance, particularly if the motifs are sizeable.

Attach the fixtures above the window at the points you established at the measuring stage, checking that the exact distance between them will marry with the width of the fabric. It is normal to fix the square-footed bracket to the left of the window and the round-footed one to the right, which allows the blind to roll up behind the roller at the top. This means that the wrong side of the fabric will be visible round the roller when the blind is up. If you feel that this would be unaesthetic, reverse the fittings.

Next decide on the position of the batten. The alternatives are at the very bottom which is the plainer and more straightforward; or a short way from the bottom which will allow for a variety of decorative hems (see below). Saw the batten to the correct length.

For the first alternative you can either glue the batten to the wrong side as in fig 1, glue its other side and then roll the bottom up so that the batten is enclosed (weight it while the glue dries); or you can make a casing by turning up a hem on the wrong side and stitching across to fit snugly round the batten (fig 2). You don't need to form a double hem as the material won't fray, but you do need to make the stitching absolutely straight.

If you decide upon a decorative hem, make the casing about 10 cm up from the bottom of the blind – this measurement will depend on the overall proportions. If you don't want to interrupt an obvious pattern, sew a gusset of extra material to the back of the blind – again the stitching must be absolutely straight.

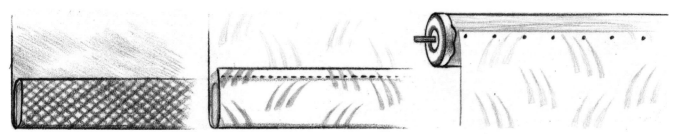

1 *Either glue the batten to the wrong side of the roller blind, and roll the blind up to enclose the batten and the raw bottom edge*

2 *or sew a casing just wide enough to take the batten snugly. You don't need to make a double hem as the material won't fray.*

3 *Fix the blind squarely to the roller by hammering in tacks.*

4 *Roman blinds pull up into neat pleats.*

To fix the top end of the fabric to the roller, draw a line across the roller (if there isn't one marked already), preferably with the help of someone holding it steady to ensure accuracy. Line up the fabric with this guideline and secure it with adhesive tape as a trial run. The fabric should be stuck wrong side up if the square pin occurs on the left, right side up if the square pin occurs on the right.

When you are happy that the blind lies squarely tack the fabric to the roller with small tacks (these may come with the kit) – see fig 3.

Form any decorative bottom edging (see below) before screwing the cord holder to the centre of the batten, following the kit's instructions.

Roman blinds

Roman blinds are easy to make and do not require specially stiffened fabric. They are lined, and pull up into pleats at the top of the window by a cord mechanism sewn to the back of the blind (fig 4).

You will need enough fabric and lining material to cover the window frame, plus 2.5 cm at each side and a total of 15 cm added to the length for the heading and hem. Adjust the total if a large pattern will need centring or lining up with the bottom. You will also have to calculate how many rings (brass or plastic) you will need given that there will be one every 15 cm

Curtains and blinds

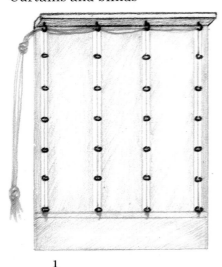

1

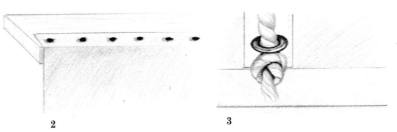

2

3

1 The drawing shows how the rows of rings attached to binding tape lie straight horizontally and vertically over the back of the Roman blind; the cords all converge at one side.

2 The Roman blind is fixed to the head board by a row of tacks.

3 Anchor the bottom of each cord by knotting it under the bottom ring.

vertically up the blind and one every 30 cm across the blind. Also buy enough binding tape for the number of rows of rings across the blind multiplied by the height of the blind, measured from the batten (see fig 1).

Other requirements are enough non-stretch cord double the height of each row *plus* the distance from the top of each row to the side (again, see fig 1); a screw eye large enough to take the cords (the one at the side where they all converge will probably have to be larger); a cleat for winding the cords round when the blind is raised; a metal rod or wooden batten the width of the blind; a piece of wood measuring 2.5 cm × 5 cm × the width of the blind; two brackets and screws for fixing the heading board to the top of the window frame.

Cut out the fabric and the lining, making sure first that they are completely straight. The dimensions will be the height and width of the finished blind plus 5 cm for the side turnings and 15 cm for the top and bottom. Pin them together, right sides facing, and tack round all sides except the top; check that there is no slack before machine-sewing 12 mm in from the edges. Trim the corners, turn the bag inside out and press it.

Lay the blind out flat with the lining uppermost. Using the batten as a ruler mark in faint pencil two lines parallel to the bottom, the first 14 cm from the bottom, and the next just far enough away so that when the casing is sewn the batten or rod will fit comfortably but not loosely within it.

Then draw vertical lines across the blind, at intervals of about 30 cm, starting at the casing and continuing up to the top. The width of the blind will dictate the actual distance between the rows, but there should be a row 1 cm from each edge.

Tack the tape along these lines, turning in the raw edges at top and bottom. Machine-stitch through all thicknesses down each side of the tape. Slipstitch the ends together, then machine the horizontal batten lines.

Handstitch on the rings at intervals of 15 cm up each row making sure that they are quite level across the blind (fig 1).

Then unpick one side seam of the casing, slot in the batten or rod and slipstitch the ends back together.

Fix the screw eyes to the underside of the head board so that they will line up with the rows of rings on the blind. The larger eye should be at the right hand side as you face the window. Then hammer in tacks through the top of the blind to the top of the board (fig 2).

Cut the cords to the correct length. This will be double the height of the blind plus the distance along the top from that particular row to the larger screw eye. Then thread the cords through the rings, knotting each one below the bottom ring (fig 3). Knot them all together just beyond the larger screw eye and again at their ends, trimming them to the same length.

Fix the brackets and the heading board above the window, and screw the cleat to the wall at a comfortable height. Draw up the blind into its folds. It is best if you can keep the blind raised for a couple of days to set the pleats.

Austrian or festoon blinds

These blinds work on the same principle as Roman blinds but are not usually lined. They pull up into soft scalloped frills, and the heading is either gathered or pleated, as on a curtain, and the hem sometimes given an extra frill (fig 4).

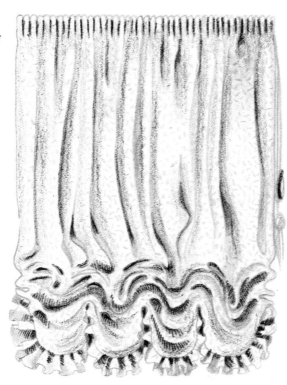

4 *Austrian blinds combine the principles of conventional curtains in their heading and of Roman blinds in their working mechanism.*

Measure the width of the window, and double it, adding on 3 or 4 cm to the total for side hems. Then measure the height of the window and add 20 cm to allow for the heading and hem. Add on another 10 cm if you want to have a frill.

From these measurements you will be able to estimate the amount of fabric to buy. If you need to join widths, use French seams as they are the neatest.

You will also need plastic or brass rings, 2 cm wide binding tape, non-stretch cord, screw eyes, a piece of wood for the heading board, two brackets to mount the board, and a cleat – all these are exactly as for Roman blinds. A further requirement is heading tape for gathered or pencil pleats to the width of the window plus turnings, and an appropriate number of hooks and gliders (ask the sales assistant).

Cut out the fabric to the dimensions you decided on, and turn in double 1.5 cm side hems. Sew the frill to the bottom edge if you are having one, or hem the bottom in conjunction with the sides so that you can mitre the corners.

To make a frill, cut a length of fabric 10 cm deep and twice the finished width of the blind – in this case, four times the width of the window. If necessary join strips in an ordinary flat seam; press the turnings open. Press the frill in half lengthwise, wrong sides together, and gather along the raw edges. Draw the frill up in even gathers to fit the blind and pin it along the bottom edge, right sides together, so that the blind extends a centimetre beyond the frill. Machine-sew 1 cm in from the edge of the frill. Trim the frill's edge, then turn the other edge down over the seam to neaten it.

Continue as for Roman blinds. The lowest rings will be 7 cm from the bottom or from where the frill's seam is.

Sew on the heading tape to the wrong side of the blind before threading through the cords, and gather the tape up to fit the width of the blind.

Beds and bedding

This chapter contains some of the least complicated projects in the book – and some of the trickiest and most lavish. If you are completely new to sewing or soft furnishing, you may gain confidence and enthusiasm by starting off with a plain pillowcase in a pretty or jazzy fabric to match your bedroom; or you could tackle a simple throw-over bedspread or a duvet cover. The other bedspreads and even some of the bed hangings are not as difficult as they appear, but it would be best to leave the corona and drapes until you're happy with the basic techniques.

The savings in making sheets and pillowcases are not great but your bed may be an unusual size or you may want to choose your own fabric in a particular colour or pattern. Pillowcases can look attractive in the same patterned material as the sheets or duvet cover. Cotton or a cotton/polyester mix are the fabrics generally used and you can of course add decorative borders, frills or lace edgings. Making them up is relatively simple.

As a postscript we have included instructions for making curtains for a dressing-table and for covering a waste-paper bin – both items that you may want to bring into your bedroom's decorating scheme.

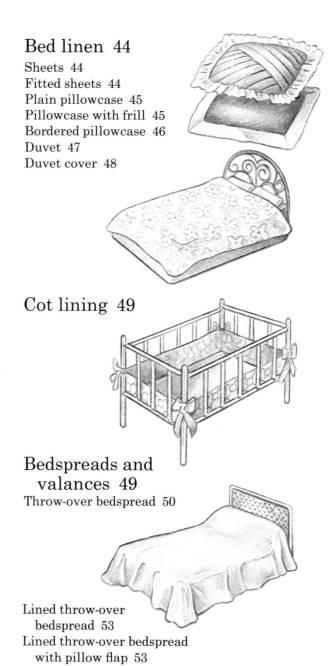

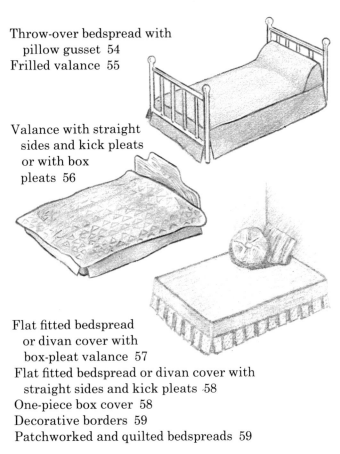

Headboards 59

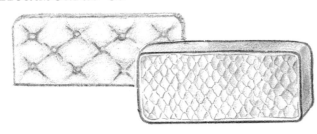

Bed linen

Sheets

First determine the width of fabric you need. Sheeting comes in a width of 228 cm which is generally wide enough to avoid uncomfortable seams.

Measure across the bed and add double the depth of the mattress. Add 45 cm for each side as a tuck-under. For the length, measure the length of the bed, plus twice the depth of the mattress, plus 30 cm for the head end, and 45 cm for a tuck-under at the bottom. Add an allowance for a double 7.5 cm hem at the top, and a double 5 cm hem at the bottom.

Cut out the material and machine-sew both the hems. Repeat for a pair. You could give the top sheet a decorative lace or broderie anglaise edging.

Fitted sheets

You may want the bottom sheet of a pair to fit the mattress to prevent it rucking up uncomfortably.

The elasticated fitting is used on all four corners of the sheet to pull it taut. This is where you can really benefit from doing the work yourself by achieving a perfect fit for your particular bed.

Measure the length and width of the mattress. Add to these measurements twice the depth of the mattress. Add 11.5 cm to each side and end to allow for the part tucked underneath the mattress (10 cm) and for hem allowances of 1.5 cm. Buy sheeting to these measurements, and a metre of 1 cm wide elastic. Cut out the fabric.

Mark in pins at all the corners a square with sides measuring the mattress depth plus 10 cm (fig 1). Cut out and machine-stitch the corners, right sides together. Trim off the excess fabric and neaten the edges, best done by machine-zigzagging (fig 2).

Press up a hem on the wrong side all the way round the sheet, taking 5 mm on the first turning and 2 cm on the second. Machine-stitch along all four sides but start and finish 15 cm from the corners. Also stitch round the corners but leave 2 cm gaps so that you'll be able to insert the elastic (fig 3). Cut the elastic into four lengths of 25 cm each. Insert one into each corner with a bodkin and stitch the ends level with the openings so that the corners are gathered up.

1 *To make fitted sheets mark in pins squares of 10 cm at each corner.*

2 *Cut out and machine-stitch the corners, right sides together. Trim and neaten the edges.*

3 *Turn up a double hem on the wrong side all the way round, leaving gaps at each corner so that you can insert elastic to draw up the sheets to fit the mattress.*

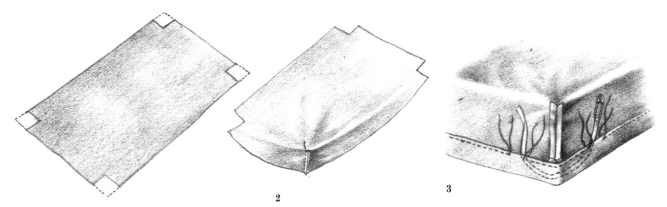

1

2

3

4 *Plain and bordered pillowcases.*

and press the seams. Stitch again 5 mm in from the edge to form a French seam. Turn and press the finished pillowcase.

If you cut the fabric in two or three sections the seams must fall where the fabric folds over to make the housewife pocket, and/or at the other end. Join the sections with French seams. Continue as for the one-piece pillowcase.

Pillowcase with frill

A frill adds a decorative touch to a pillow and is popular when used with a duvet since the pillows are visible during the day. This type of pillowcase is made from three sections, plus the frill. The separate pocket section should be cut to the width of the top and bottom sections and to a depth of 16 cm.

Start by making the frill itself. Its length will be $1\frac{1}{2}$ to 2 times the perimeter of the pillow. You may find it convenient to economise on cutting by making up the frill from shorter widths. Seams do not matter as they will be unobtrusive. Sew the widths end to end, open out the seams and press them. The width of the frill itself should be a doubled 2.5 cm, plus 2.5 cm for the seam, so a total of 7.5 cm.

Sew the short ends of the long strip together, right sides together, and open and press them. Fold the fabric lengthwise, wrong sides together, into a continuous tube, and sew two lines of gathering stitch all round, 1.25 cm and 1 cm in from the raw edges.

Gather up the frill to the outer dimensions of the case. Pin it to one of the main sections, right sides and raw edges together. Adjust the frill to give a fairly even gather all round except on the corners, where it is important to have plenty of fullness or the finished frill will not stand out well from the pillow.

Sew the frill to the pillow all round along the line of the gathering stitch nearest to the edge of the frill. Take the pocket section and give it a

Plain pillowcase

The pillowcase has a pocket or 'housewife' which holds the pillow in position. You can make the case from one, two or three sections, depending on whether you are making the case from small pieces or a generous length. Not all manufactured pillows come in a standard size so you will need to measure your pillow. For a one-piece case, measure the length and width of the pillow. The fabric should be the width of the pillow plus 8 cm for turnings and room for getting the pillow in and out easily. The length should be twice the length of the pillow plus 23 cm for the pocket, turnings and room for manoeuvre. Try to cut the piece so that one of the short ends has a selvedge.

Press under the opposite end by 6.5 cm and stitch under 5 mm of that, close to the edge, to make a double hem. Fold the selvedge end over, wrong sides together, to make a pocket 15 cm long, and over that fold up the hemmed end. Also wrong sides together, stitch the side edges half a centimetre in from the edge, and trim the seams to half that. Turn the pillowcase wrong side out

double hem down one of its lengths allowing 18 mm for the turnings. Lay it over the frilled section of the pillowcase, right sides together, and sew along the end seam (fig 1). Press it right sides out.

1 *For a frilled pillow-case, attach the frill to the right side of one of the main sections. Then attach the pocket to the assembly, right sides together, keeping the frill itself clear.*

Make a double hem across one end of the other section with 18 mm turnings. Place the two pieces of fabric right sides together and stitch round the sides and bottom 1 cm in from the raw edges. Keep the frill carefully tucked in so that you do not catch it in the seams. You cannot use a French seam if you are inserting a frill so you will have to trim the corners and neaten the seams with machine zigzagging or overcasting by hand.

Bordered pillowcase

Again, you will have to make this type of pillowcase from three pieces of material (four, if the border is contrasting). The bottom piece should be the width and length of the pillow plus 8 cm for turnings and room for getting the pillow in and out. The top should have an extra 14 cm added to the width and length which allows for borders of 6 cm and a total of 2 cm of turnings. The pocket section should be the width of the bottom section and 16 cm deep.

First machine-sew a narrow hem along one of the short ends of the bottom piece, then along one of the long ends of the pocket.

Fold under all the edges of the larger top piece by 1 cm and press down another 7 cm. Mitre the corners and sew down the mitring to form a neat border. Take the pocket piece and with wrong sides together slip the raw edges between the folded border at one end. Tack it and then machine zigzag (or sew by hand) only along the long edge.

Now place the prepared bottom section on the top piece, wrong sides together, so that the hem is at the pocket end. Insert all the raw edges evenly between the border. Tack them in position and zigzag stitch to finish. All the raw edges are thus hidden within the border (fig 2).

If you want the border to be in a contrasting material cut four strips the length of the pillow plus twice the depth of the border plus 1 cm for two 1 cm turnings. Each piece should be about 14 cm wide (which will give a border of 6 cm plus a total of 2 cm for turnings). The top and bottom sections of the case will have the same dimensions this time.

Fold the strips in half lengthwise, and mitre and stitch the corners, right sides together. Turn and press the border, and slip it between the prepared main sections of the pillowcase (again you will have to use three pieces of fabric in order to accommodate the border). The inside edges of this version will be raw so you should machine zigzag them or overcast them by hand.

Instead of fabric strips you could use lengths of ruched lace and slip a single layer of it between the top and bottom of the pillowcase.

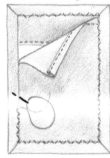

2 *The raw edge of the pocket and then the raw edges of the top section of the pillowcase are all contained within the border.*

Duvet

The fashion for duvets (continental quilts) in recent years has led to competition and the reduction of prices to a reasonable level, so you may think it worthwhile to make your own duvet only if you have an unusually large bed or long legs. Alternatively, you may want to convert an old eiderdown but you will have to supplement the filling as an equivalent duvet needs more down. If you do decide to make a duvet it is quite simple and relatively economical.

The duvet consists of a channelled bag filled with goose or duck down, feathers, or synthetic material. Goose down is considered the best and most luxurious because it is the lightest, but synthetic filling is the cheapest, easiest to handle, and washable (fig 5). The bag is divided into compartments to prevent the feathers shaking down into one end. Its light weight and flexibility enable it to sink around the sleeper's body, eliminating pockets of cold air and providing perfect insulation. The thickness of the layer of filling also stops heat loss and, best of all, there is no bed-making: a quick shake of the duvet and the bed is made.

You can buy the type of filling you prefer at a good upholstery supplies shop. The fabric used for the duvet itself must be a downproof cambric which is waxed on one side to stop the sharp quills poking through. The cambric is covered by a second bag which is taken off for washing.

To decide upon the size of the duvet, measure the bed from top to bottom and from side to side. Add at least 20 cm at the bottom of the bed for the overhang, and at least 40 cm to the width measurement for the overhang at the two sides. There is no tuck-in on a duvet if you use it properly. It relies on its weight to seal up the gaps at the side of the bed and if you have insufficient overhang, you may well find that the edges are not sealed. To all these measurements, add a further 2.5 cm at the top, bottom, and both sides for the seam turnings. Cut two pieces of cambric to these measurements.

Sew them with French seams around the two sides and top. If the cambric is too small to make the bag from one width, sew widths together using a French seam, joining right sides (unwaxed) together first. Trim the seam turnings, turn the bag inside out and machine-sew round the seams again.

Divide the bag into tubes of an equal width as near to 20 cm wide as possible, running lengthwise down the bed. Mark the sewing lines with

3 *Divide the bag into equal channels to run the length of the bed.*

4 *While you are filling the duvet, keep the filled tubes closed with pegs.*

5 *Down, feather, and synthetic fillings for duvets.*

3

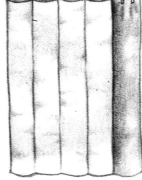

4

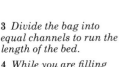

5

chalk and sew down them (fig 3 on page 47). The bulk may present some problems in your sewing machine, but if you sew from each side towards the centre, folding the remainder of the fabric into a neat roll as you go, you should be able to cope. A refinement if you are going to fill the duvet with feathers would be to wax down the stitching with a piece of beeswax to prevent the quills poking up through the sewing holes.

You can now fill the tubes. You need enough to stop most of the heat loss from your body but you will defeat the object if you pack the tubes so tightly that they become stiff and inflexible. One tube of average length will take about 250 g of filling.

Down and feathers are unruly objects to have flying about and they are also expensive. If you do lose any they are better off outside so you might find it preferable to carry out the filling operation in the garden on a still day. A washing line is a useful accessory. (Another possible place, second best, would be the bathroom with the door shut.) Peg the duvet case at the seams along the washing line so that you can use both hands while the openings at the top of the tubes stay open. Divide the filling into as many portions as there are tubes, each weighing about 250 g. Contain them temporarily in large polythene bags closed with pegs.

Take one bag, plunge your hand in, take a firm handful of filling or feathers and stuff it right down into the first tube before you release it. That way you should be able to keep losses to a minimum.

When you have used up the bagful close off the opening to the tube with a peg or two, and go on to the next (fig 3 on page 47). When you have distributed the filling and have a nicely fat duvet without any stiffness, and all the holes are closed off with pegs, take the duvet down from the washing line, tack and sew (and wax) the last seam. You could enclose the raw edges with bias binding to neaten them.

Duvet cover

By comparison, after all this effort, making an outer cover for the duvet is simple. Buy polyester-cotton sheeting (which comes in extra wide widths) as large as the duvet, adding a 10 cm margin to both the width and length to avoid restricting the duvet itself. Sew it round the top and two sides making a French seam. Turn in the allowance at the bottom edge into a double 2 cm seam, stitch up about 10 cm at each side and attach 'poppered' tape or Velcro to close the opening.

Cot lining

Washable and reversible cotton/polyester quilting is by far the best material for lining a cot as its padding will prevent the baby hurting itself against the cot bars and it will keep out draughts.

You will need fabric to go round the four sides of the cot but it need not go right up to the top of the bars – about 30 cm high is easily enough to protect the baby's head. The base of the cot lining goes under the mattress so can be made from lining material, calico or other washable left-over fabric. You will also need 2.5 m of ribbon to match the quilting.

Cut the fabric for the four sides and the base, including seam allowances of 1.25 cm. Join the two short ends to one of the long sides so that the right side of the seams will face in towards the cot. Trim the seams, press them and cover them with binding to neaten them. Also bind the raw edges of the two end pieces and round the top edge.

Sew the base to these three sides, right side of quilting to under side of the base – all the raw edges will eventually be hidden by the mattress. Turn the structure so that the seams are inside.

Bedspreads and valances

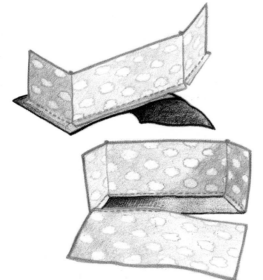

Sew the base of the cot lining to the two short sides and one of the long sides, right side of quilting to wrong side of base. Then turn the structure so that the right side of the seams are to the inside.

The traditional type of bedspread, a well-constructed fabric cover designed to conceal the bedclothes and form part of the bedroom decoration, has fallen rather out of fashion in recent years. Widespread use of the duvet, itself contained in a decorative bag, has done away with the need for a further cover. However, many people still prefer sheets and blankets, making some kind of bed covering desirable.

The traditional bedspread offers an almost limitless range of design possibilities. The instructions here cover a variety of types from a simple throw-over bedspread to more complicated fitted styles. By adapting them you will be able to achieve exactly the effect you want, whether you are designing your bedspread or copying one in a magazine or shop display.

A valance covers the base of the bed when a duvet or a half-length throw-over bedspread is used. It can be made from the same material as the sheets and duvet cover, probably polyester-cotton sheeting in the same or a contrasting colour, or a heavier fabric. The part of the valance that covers the base of the bed under the mattress is never seen so can be made from lining

Then deal with the remaining long side, first binding its side and top edges and then sewing it to the open edge of the base, wrong sides together. The fourth side has to be unattached except at the base so that when the cot side is let down it doesn't get in the way.

Cut the ribbon into 12 equal lengths (about 20 cm long) and attach six in three pairs down each long side of the cot lining – at each corner and at or near the middle to correspond with a cot bar. The ribbons are tied round the bars to keep the lining in place.

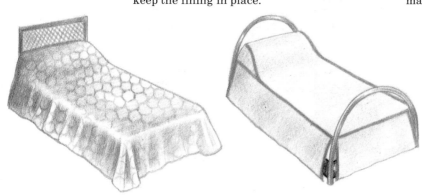

fabric, calico, or a piece of old sheeting as long as it is not worn. If it stretched out right to the sides of the bed it might just be visible between the mattress and the base so it is surrounded by a narrow border in the same fabric as the sides.

There are various styles: a simple gathered frill, box-pleats, or kick pleats at the corners of a straight-sided valance. It can go all round the bed, or just round the sides and bottom if the head of the bed is against a wall.

Throw-over bedspread

One of the simplest and most effective bedspreads consists of a piece of fabric cut to size, sewn, and draped over the bed, almost touching the floor. If you want to have a valance round the base of the bed, the cover can hang to just below the top of the valance.

If you want to take the bedspread off the bed at night any weight of fabric is suitable though a washable and crease-resistant one would be best. A plain or printed linen, cotton or synthetic

fabric would be the cheapest. Brocades and satins produce luxurious results but if you are new to sewing it would be wise to avoid these expensive materials. Otherwise the finest fabric you can afford is well invested in a bedspread. Cotton lace comes in very wide widths so you don't have to join any seams. If you intend to use the spread as part of the bedclothes, washable quilted fabric would be a good choice since it is particularly crease-resistant and very warm.

Measuring the bed

Start by measuring the bed (fig 1). Make up the bed with the usual bedclothes and pillows in place. If you only measure the mattress the bedspread won't be long enough when it has to cover all the bedding.

Using a fabric tape, measure the width over the bed from the floor one side to the floor the other. Add 20 cm to give a double 5 cm hem at each side, and 5 cm for each seam. Subtract 2 cm from the total to give a 1 cm clearance at each

1 *It is important that the bed's measurements are taken over the made-up bed – otherwise the finished bedspread will hang short.*

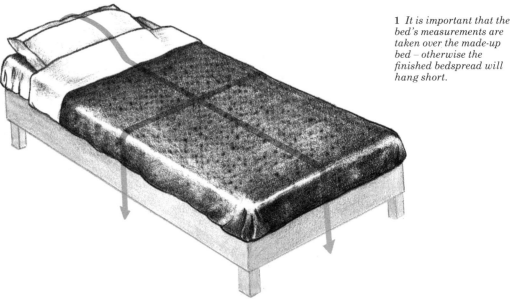

side, just enough to stop the bedspread brushing the floor. If you are making a half-spread for use with a valance, measure over the made-up bed down to a point 10 cm below the bottom of the mattress.

Measuring the length is slightly more complicated. Start at the head of the bed by the pillows, and measure along the length down to the floor at the foot (or to 10 cm below the bottom of the mattress). Add 10 cm for a double 5 cm hem there, plus 18 cm to tuck down behind the head end of the bed, and a further 5 cm for a double 2.5 cm turning at the top. The measurements are slightly flexible in that the depth of the hemming is not critical all round and no attempt is made to accommodate the bulk of the pillows. You will find that this simple design of bedspread falls neatly even if a little way off the floor at each side near the head end.

Estimating the fabric

All beds take more than one width of fabric. A single bed, say 75 cm wide and 37.5 cm high, would require a 150 cm width of material plus hem and seam allowances. This would come comfortably from two widths of most fabrics, so you would need to buy fabric amounting to twice the total length. If you choose a material with a large pattern allow extra for matching, about the depth of one pattern repeat for each width.

For a large double bed, perhaps 135 cm wide and 67.5 cm off the floor, the total width of fabric would need to be 270 cm, plus hem and seam allowances. Clearly you could not form this from two widths of fabric, even using a wide weave of 135 cm, so you would have to buy three times the length measurement. Unfortunately this involves a lot of waste, but the problem is unavoidable.

Whether you are making a single or a double bedspread it is important to have a complete panel down the centre of the bed with seams to either side, avoiding an unsightly centre join. Cut across the width to the required length, starting each piece from the same point in the pattern if the material has an obvious repeat. For a single bedspread, fold the material in half lengthwise and cut along the fold. Cut one of the pieces in half along its length. The halves will be sewn to the sides of the full centre panel width. You may need to reduce the width of this centre section so that the seams fall in appropriate places – ie not down the vertical sides.

Making up the cover

Join the lengths right sides together, using a flat seam with a 2 cm allowance. Cut the selvedge off if the fabric is glazed chintz. Otherwise, make notches along the selvedges at 15 cm intervals to prevent any puckering. Press the seams open and neaten the raw edges by machine zigzagging or hand overcasting. Alternatively, you could use a run-and-fell seam.

There are two choices for the treatment of corners. If you sew the hems all round as they are, mitring the corners, you will find that there is a great flap of excess. This is acceptable but you may prefer to avoid the corners trailing by trimming the fabric to meet the floor. It will hang in ample folds because there will still be surplus fabric but the hems themselves will neatly touch the floor all round.

To form the cutting line for rounded corners, lay the bedspread fabric on the bed. Take hold of the fabric at one of the bottom corners and ease it down to the point where it meets the floor. Mark this point with a pin. Continue marking with a pin round the fabric from one side to the other until you have a curved line of pins all round the excess fabric. Trim the fabric to the line of the curve (fig 1 overleaf). To cut the other side, fold the fabric in half and follow the first cutting line (fig 2 overleaf). The bedspread will now fit to the floor neatly on both sides of the bed.

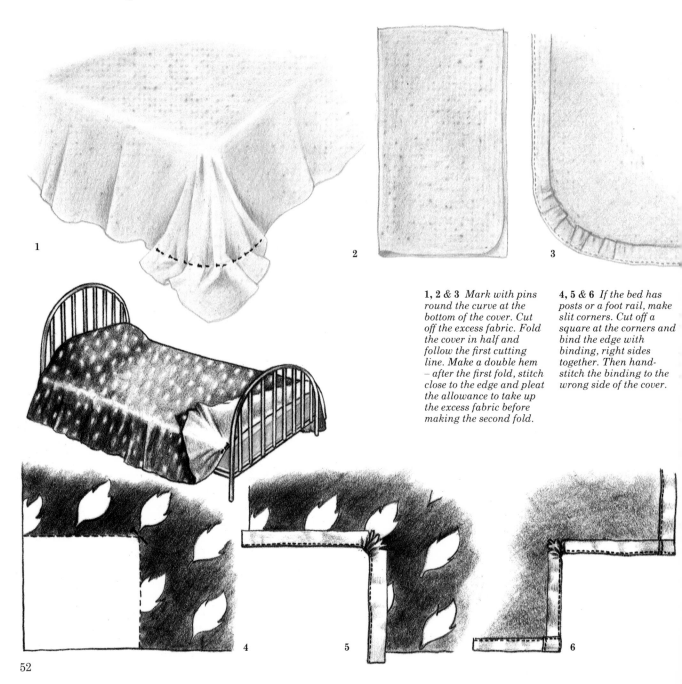

1, 2 & 3 *Mark with pins round the curve at the bottom of the cover. Cut off the excess fabric. Fold the cover in half and follow the first cutting line. Make a double hem – after the first fold, stitch close to the edge and pleat the allowance to take up the excess fabric before making the second fold.*

4, 5 & 6 *If the bed has posts or a foot rail, make slit corners. Cut off a square at the corners and bind the edge with binding, right sides together. Then hand-stitch the binding to the wrong side of the cover.*

Turn in and press 2.5 cm all round the bedspread. If you are making rounded corners, stitch close to the foldline and pleat or notch the allowance to take up the excess fabric (fig 3). Fold the material over again to form a double hem. Mitre the corners at the top of the bed.

The bedspread is now finished. It should tuck neatly down behind the pillows at the top and hang comfortably just off the floor or over the top of the valance all round.

If the bed has posts or a foot rail you will need to make slit corners (figs 4, 5 and 6). When you have joined the panels together, lay the cover on the bed and pin the corner. Remove the cover and cut off the corner leaving a 1 cm seam allowance. Cut a bias strip of the main fabric, sew it to the cover, right sides together, and clip the curves as you turn it under. Handstitch the remaining edge to the wrong side of the cover.

If the bed has a solid board at the foot, measure the length of the top panel so that there is an allowance for tucking down between the mattress and the board. The bottom corners will be mitred.

The flap to cover the llows is cut and sewn parately.

The main cover lies flat der the pillows, and e flap returns over them tuck underneath.

Lined throw-over bedspread

The advantages of lining a bedspread are warmth (especially if you use a quilted lining) and a neater, crease-resistant finish. Use a lining fabric that is compatible in terms of washing or dry-cleaning with the main fabric. Cut it out and sew the seams exactly as for the main cover. With wrong sides together lockstitch the cover and lining together along the seams (see page 21). Turn in the lining, tack it to the bedspread 2.5 cm in from the edge all round and slipstitch it into position.

An alternative method would be to place the lining and cover right sides together and machine-stitch all round the edge leaving a 60 cm gap along the top edge. Trim square corners diagonally and pleat or notch round corners. Turn the bedspread right side out and press it. Slipstitch the opening together.

Throw-over bedspread with pillow flap

If you use one or even two large pillows, their bulk can throw the line of the bedspread out of balance unless some provision is made for it. One simple solution is to add a flap (or 'scarf') to the top of the bedspread. The cover itself lies flat under the pillows but the flap returns over them and then tucks underneath (fig 8).

If the bedspread were made from a single piece of fabric, the part showing over the pillows would be the wrong side of the fabric, so the flap is cut separately and sewn on in reverse (fig 7).

Measure the length of the bed, without pillows, from the head of the bed to the floor, remembering the hem allowances. Replace the pillows and measure loosely from the top of the bed, over the pillows and back under them for about 20 cm, to determine the length of the extra flap. The flap should be wide enough at least to cover the pillows or even to reach the floor on

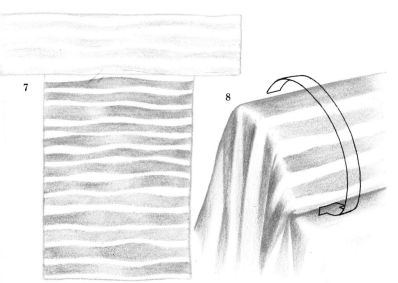

7

8

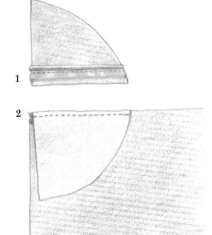

1

2

3

1 *Sew a short length of piping to the bottom edge of the gusset.*

2 *Sew the gusset to the skirt, right sides together.*

3 & 4 *For a neat finish, the piping of the curved part of the gusset should lie over the piping of the lower straight edge.*

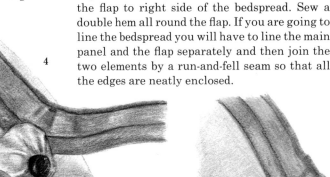

4

each side, so that it hangs in an attractive fold. Take care when you cut the fabric that any prominent design is centrally placed. Sew the flap to the main part of the cover, wrong side of the flap to right side of the bedspread. Sew a double hem all round the flap. If you are going to line the bedspread you will have to line the main panel and the flap separately and then join the two elements by a run-and-fell seam so that all the edges are neatly enclosed.

Throw-over bedspread with pillow gusset

An alternative way of accommodating the pillows is to sew a gusset into the side of the bedspread. The bedspread will then fit neatly over the bed and pillows together. If you have a gusset the rest of the design is usually tailored to the bed's dimensions too and incorporates piping into all the seams. The sides can be gathered, plain with kick pleats at the bottom corners (see page 58), or box-pleated (see page 57).

You will have to estimate the shape of the gusset to fit the pillows. A useful measurement that would accommodate most single pillows would be 12 cm high and 40 cm long, rising in a generous curve to match the curve of the pillow. The dimensions can be increased for two pillows or one very full one. Add a 2.5 cm seam allowance round the curve, and 5 cm seam allowance along the straight bottom and at the end hem. You may find it helpful to make a paper pattern of the area before you cut the material. Remember to cut one left-hand and one right-hand gusset.

When you are measuring for the top panel of the cover add on 25 or 30 cm to allow for the height of the pillows and for a little to tuck behind them. If you are not lining the bedspread make all seams 5 cm wide to allow for neatening; otherwise they can be 2.5 cm wide. The measurements for the frill, straight or box-pleated sides will be from the top of mattress (with normal bedclothes in position) down to 1 cm above the floor, plus 5 cm for the hem and 1 cm for the seam at the top.

Prepare the sides first. Then deal with the gusset. If you are using interlining tack or iron it to the wrong side of the gusset, and press the seam allowances, especially round the curved part of the gusset. Turn in and sew the 5 cm end allowance into a 2.5 cm double hem.

You will need enough piping to go right round the side and bottom edges of the bed and along the curved part of the gusset (see page 80 for how to make it). First sew a short length of piping to the bottom straight edge of the gusset (fig 1). Then sew the gusset to the skirt of the bedspread, right side to right side (fig 2), and turn over the seam allowance to tidy up the raw edges (see page 31). Next sew piping to the curved part of the gusset and continue this piping right round the skirt of the bedspread. The piping of the curved part of the gusset should lie over the piping of the lower straight edge for a neater finish (figs 3 & 4).

Lastly, you can machine the skirt and gusset to the top panel of the bedspread. Clip the curves, particularly round the top of the gusset.

If you want to line a fitted cover, cut a lining for the top panel, gussets and sides. Assemble the pieces and apply the lining to the cover wrong side to wrong side. If it is a full lining, lockstitch along the seams (see page 21), then turn and press under all the raw edges of the lining, tack them to the cover and hem them in position. Otherwise turn in and press the half-lining (one that lines the top panel only) and sew it down

over the seams of the cover to hide them.

If you are not lining the cover, double-hem the top edge of the main panel, and hem round the frill or the sides.

Frilled valance

The instructions given are for a three-sided valance. Take off the mattress to measure the length and width of the base of the bed. The base panel will have these measurements plus 4 cm for turnings, plus an extra 25 cm for a large flap to tuck in at the top.

The valance is made from a long gathered strip of fabric to go round the sides and bottom of the bed. Measure the depth of the base from its top to the floor. Add 2 cm for the seam allowance at the top, and 4 cm for a double 2 cm hem at the bottom. Subtract 1 cm for clearance off the floor. This measurement is the height of the frill. To look right, the pattern must run vertically so you should cut the strips from several widths of the fabric joined together. Measure the length of the bed, double it to allow for the two sides, and add the width of the bed. Double this total to accommodate the gather. You can now calculate how many widths you will have to cut and join.

For the three borders cut three strips of the same fabric as the frill, each about 20 cm wide (15 cm plus two seam allowances of 2.5 cm), two the length and one the width of the mattress (each plus 2.5 cm for turnings).

Tack the wrong side of the border lengths to the right side of the bottom panel, outer edges together, press under 2.5 cm on the inside edges of the border, mitring the corners, and then machine round (fig 5).

Sew together the lengths of fabric for the frill. Press the seams open and neaten the edges. Mark a sewing line 1.5 cm from the top edge all along the strip. Double the length of the bed and mark off this measurement from one end of the strip by a tailor's tack. Then double the width of the bed

The valance base lies under the mattress but needs a border in the same fabric as the frill so that the edges of the centre panel can't be seen. Tack the border lengths, right side up, round the centre panel, outer edges together. Press under 2.5 cm at the inside edges, mitre the corners, and machine round. Then go on to attach the frill.

1 *Draw up the gathering threads on one section of the frill until it is as long as the bed ; wind them round a pin to secure them.*

2 *Tack the frill to the base panel, right sides together. Start the frill 25 cm from the top end of the base panel.*

3 *Add any piping at this stage.*

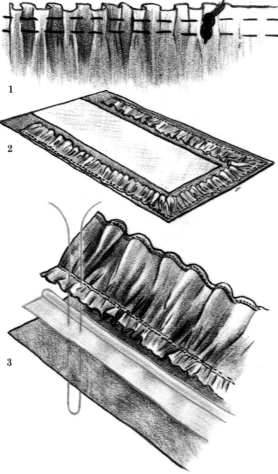

1

2

3

you are hand-sewing) away from the first line nearer the edge.

Gather up one side of the frill as far as the first tailor's tack. Draw the threads up until the side is as long as the bed and wind them securely round a pin (fig 1). Match the position of the pin on the frill to the corner of the base fabric. Tack and then sew the frill and the base panel together, right side to right side, with a 2 cm seam allowance (fig 2). (The beginning of the frill should start 25 cm from the top end of the lining fabric where the flap at the head of the bed will be.) If you are having piping add it at this stage (fig 3). Next draw up the gathers and sew the bottom of the valance, and finally the third side again, as far as the point 25 cm from the end. Grade the seams and neaten the edges. Turn in and slipstitch the unsewn ends of the border, and hem round the flap.

You can now fit the valance to the bed. Adjust it so that the corners fall neatly into place at the bottom, and smooth it out towards the top. Tuck the flap down behind the head end of the bed. If you wish, you can slipstitch the sides of the flap to the vertical ends of the frill so that the cover does not get dislodged. You can also sew on tapes to tie round the inner sides of the bed legs to ensure that the valance stays in place.

Valance with straight sides and kick pleats or with box pleats

Make the valance as if you were constructing the flat fitted bedspread in either of its variations described next in the chapter. Measure the depth of the side panels or pleats from the top of the mattress base. Instructions for the base panel under the mattress are as for the frilled valance on the previous page. You will probably want to pipe the edges round the mattress base in keeping with the more tailored line of the pleats or kick pleats.

and mark off that position from the first mark. These are the positions of the corners at the bottom of the bed. Turn up and stitch a double 2 cm hem all the way round, and hem what will be the vertical ends of the frill.

Gather along the sewing line as far as the first mark. Repeat along the part marked for the width, then along the final length. Sew a second row of gathering along the same lengths, the width of the sewing-machine foot (about 25 mm if

Flat fitted bedspread or divan cover with box-pleat valance

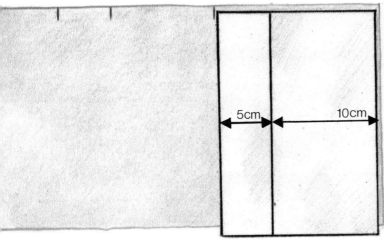

5cm   10cm

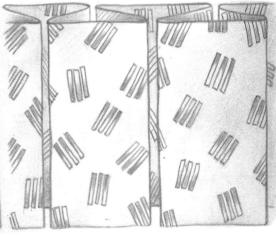

4 *Make a template the width and depth of the pleats you want. Mark the position on the back of the fabric with chalk or pins – a half-width will lie to either side of the full width. Then bring the marks together ensuring that any joins in the fabric will occur in the folds behind.*

This cover is particularly suitable for bed-sit or studio beds which turn into sofas during the day. You could have box or bolster cushions (see page 62) along the wall. It would be sensible to choose quite a heavy and hard-wearing fabric with a firm weave such as a heavy cotton/polyester mix or furnishing tweed.

For the top centre panel measure to the edges, allowing about 1 cm for the side and bottom seams and 23 cm for an 18 cm pillow tuck with a double 2.5 cm hem at the top. Join widths of fabric as necessary to make up the total width.

Place a saucer at the bottom two corners and cut along the line of its curve in order to give the bedspread gently rounded corners.

The depth of the valance will be as for a frilled valance, in other words from the base of the mattress to 1 cm above the floor. Add on 2.5 cm for the hem and just over 1 cm for the top turning. You will have to join strips of fabric (attached so that the straight grain on all pieces runs vertically) to a length that is three times the total length of the two sides and bottom of the centre panel, plus 2.5 cm for turnings. You may want the valance to go right the way round the bed in which case you should adjust the total measurement accordingly.

Turn up and press the hem of the valance before you form the pleats. Pleats of about 10 cm wide are usual, but their actual width will be dictated by the length of the edge of the bed. Divide that length into equal pleats as near as possible to 10 cm wide. This way the ends of the pleats will occur neatly at the corners.

Make a cardboard template to form accurate pleats. It should be the exact width and depth of the pleat you want. Lay the joined strips of fabric out flat, wrong side up and, using the template, mark with chalk or pins the position of the pleats all the way along. Fold the pleats as in fig 4. Seams in the strip must be hidden in the folds of the pleats. Tack the pleats in position. Sew any piping to the centre panel, and attach the valance to it. Neaten the seam or slipstitch the edges of the centre panel's lining down over the seam.

57

Flat fitted bedspread or divan cover with straight sides and kick pleats

This is another tailored variation for a cover, using less material than the box-pleated one. Again, you should choose a fairly hard-wearing fabric.

Follow the instructions for making the centre panel as given for the box-pleated version, gently rounding the corners. Cut two panels for the sides the length of the centre panel, plus 30 cm. Cut one panel for the bottom end the width of the bed also plus 30 cm. The depth of these three panels should be from the top of the mattress down to 1 cm above the floor, plus 5 cm for the hem and 1 cm for the top seam allowance.

Cut two pieces of fabric on the straight grain 30 cm long and the same depth as the side panels. Join up the sides and end, using a normal flat seam and right sides together, in this order: side panel, corner pleat, end panel, corner pleat, side panel. Take up a double 2.5 cm hem all round.

Bring the seams together for each corner so that the corner pleat sections are hidden. Make sure that each side of the pleat is an equal 14 cm. Attach any piping to the top panel. Then position the valance to it so that the pleats fall precisely at the corners. Tack and sew the seams,

Make corner kick pleats by joining the pleats between side and end panels, using an ordinary flat seam. Then bring together the seams on either side of the pleat. The folds should hang equally behind the corner.

and neaten them if you are not lining the bedspread. Hem along the top ends of the centre panel and the valance where there is the small allowance (about 18 cm) for tucking behind the pillows. Line the centre panel if you want (the valance need not be lined), hemming the edges over the main seams to neaten them.

If you want to make a valance that goes right round the bed with four kick pleats, the measurement for the side panels will be the same because the 15 cm that in the three-sided version tucks behind the pillows will go instead towards the kick pleat there. The centre panel will have the measurements of the bed plus 1 cm seam allowances all round.

One-piece box cover

This is a variation on the flat fitted bedspread but makes the sofa look even less bed-like during the day. Take the measurements for the cover over the usual bedclothes but without the pillows, following the guidelines given previously, depending on whether you want a frill, box pleats or straight sides with kick pleats, but take into account the fact that the valance goes round all four sides of the bed.

The new element in this design is the straight band round the sides of the mattress. Form this from strips of fabric (as few as possible) the depth

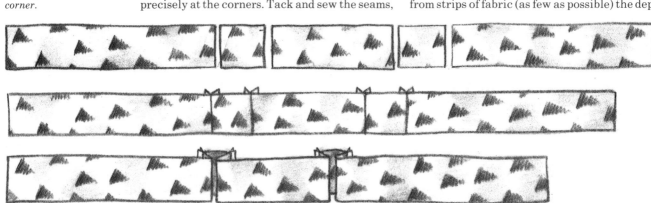

of the mattress plus two 2 cm turnings. If you want to pipe the edges tack piping all the way round the top panel. Lay the panel upside down on the mattress and pin the band to the piped edge. Join the two ends of the band at a corner and try to contrive that other joins will occur at points where the divan is against a wall. Stitch and press the seam open. Line the centre panel if you want.

Tack piping to the lower edge of the band. Form the valance and turn up its hem. Lay the piped lower edge of the band over the tacked pleats or gathers and stitch along at the base of the piping through all layers. Neaten the seams.

Decorative borders

A border in a contrasting fabric is an easy way to add unusual interest to the bedspread. You could position a border down each side of the bed from the head to the foot, or place one border on one side of the bed only. Classical in style, and fitted by cutting to a mitred shape at the corners, is the border following the outline of the bed: fit it about 20 cm from the sides and end of the bed all round. Borders must be cut on the straight grain of the fabric, turned under and pressed evenly, then sewn on to the cover by machine or hemmed invisibly by hand. Apply any decorative border before you line the bedspread.

Patchworked and quilted bedspreads

Traditionally favourite techniques in bedspread-making because of their combined economic, decorative and insulating properties are patchwork and quilting. Instructions for both are given starting on page 136.

If you want to make a quilted bedspread, whether or not with patchwork, make the simplest sort – the throw-over cover either full or half-length – as this will show off the work best.

Headboards

Headboards come in a wide variety of shapes, fabrics and forms, and should be an integral part of the design of the bed and the bedroom.

Your bed may have one already but if it has become soiled the fabric will need cleaning or even renewing. If you have recently bought a bed, it is worthwhile making a neat, washable loose cover to protect the headboard which can match the curtains, wallpaper, duvet cover or sheets.

The instructions here cover the woodwork needed to make up a headboard, padding and covering it, and making loose covers of various kinds. Take up the instructions at the point where they apply to your particular needs.

Designing the headboard

Firstly, design your headboard and examine the fixing system by which it is to be applied to your bed. A typical system involves two screw-headed bolts, with large diameter washers, over which you place slotted lengths of wood. The headboard itself is screwed to the wood. A typical system is illustrated in fig 1 overleaf, which you should adapt for your own bed.

Make sure you have enough wood above the mattress to support the headboard itself: it has to take a fair weight when leant against. The dimensions of the board depend on the design. Normally it will be the width of the bed but some designs incorporate small drawers and tables at the sides. However it is not wise to put all that weight of furniture and contents on just the two bolts screwed into the bed. For that kind of design there is another complete alternative system, but a more permanent one, which can also be used for even the simplest headboard. That is to fix the headboard to the wall, and push the bed up against it. For that you will need to

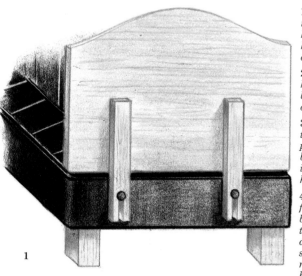

1 *Two slotted lengths of wood fixed to the headboard fit over screw-headed bolts in the base of the bed.*

2 *For a permanent headboard, plot any button design at the outset.*

3 *Drill a hole through the board at each button point. At the back of the board hammer halfway in a tack close to each hole.*

4 *Take a threaded needle from the back through board, foam and fabric, then through the button and back again, before securing the thread round the tack. Then hammer the tack home.*

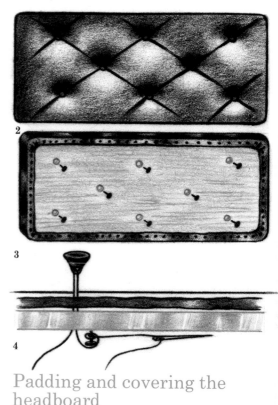

arrange a fixing system. It may be a simple screw into a plugged hole in the wall, in which case you will have to leave access space for the screw head before you finally fit the padding and covering fabric. Or you may be able to buy a spike and sleeve system at a hardware shop to slot the headboard on to the wall and take it off when you need to.

The height of the headboard depends on the design, and on the person or couple using it. Sit on the bed comfortably and find out where your head touches the wall when you are reading, drinking tea, watching the midnight movie. Design the headboard to end several centimetres higher than this (maybe even 20 cm). You can have a straight or shaped top edge. Draw the design on to 5-ply or chipboard, perhaps with the aid of a paper pattern, and cut round it. Cover the board completely with 2.5 cm thick foam cut to the shape and glued on (you could use the paper pattern again). You may want to take the foam over the top and round the edges. If so, cut out the corners to avoid a bulky overlap.

Padding and covering the headboard

If you are making a board with a permanent cover you may like to consider a button arrangement, whether a pattern of deep buttoning as on a Victorian chair, or a single button in the centre of the headboard.

Plot the button design in the early stages (fig 2) and drill a small hole through the board at each button point. At the back of the board, hammer halfway in a small tack close to the hole (fig 3). Later, whichever type of button you fit, you can push a needle through the hole, the foam and the fabric, thread on a button, push the needle back through, draw the thread tight and wrap it round the tack (fig 4), before hammering home the tack for a permanent fixing.

With the foam glued in place, you can deal with the fabric. Cut it to the shape of the board with a generous overlap all round, centring any patterns. Tauten the fabric over the board and secure it with upholsterer's tacks between the wooden fixing struts at the bottom of the board.

Smooth it out towards one side without pulling it too tight, and secure that side with more tacks. Repeat the other side. The corners are the main problem you are likely to encounter. Draw the fabric up into a flap, and tack it down. Trim off the excess fabric. At the bottom, where the struts hold the board, you will need to cut the fabric into the corners, and fold it away to conceal the raw edge. Tack the fabric down securely. Fit buttons if you are having them (see above).

For a professional finish you could cover the back with some form of lining. Fold the edges under neatly, and hammer in tacks all round at 2 cm–3 cm intervals. As an alternative you could back the board with fabric lining. Fold the edge

under and slipstitch the lining to the facing fabric all round.

There are of course many other ways of covering a headboard. Another permanent design would be to cut the foam to fit the exact shape of the board without taking it over the edge to the back. Cut the facing fabric to exactly the same size plus 1 cm all round for seam allowances, and then cut a strip wide enough to match the thickness of the foam plus that of the board, also plus 1 cm for seam allowances.

Make up piping (see page 80) in a matching or contrasting colour and sandwich it between the two parts. You could make the back in the same fabric, add a second line of piping, or finish the back in lining fabric for economy. The most likely problem is that the whole assembly may pull forwards in use, revealing the lining fabric at the back. A few tacks hammered into the lining fabric just below the top edge of the board will help to prevent this.

Loose cover for a headboard

You may find it more practical to live with an easily laundered loose cover. Make the board as described but use a cheap backing fabric.

Quilted fabric with piped seams looks attractive and is very comfortable. Cut the fabric and a lining for the back to the same dimensions as for the permanent cover. Remember to add on 1 cm all round for the turnings. You will also need a gusset strip to fit round the top and sides (again, remember the seam allowances). Place this strip to the front piece, right sides together, inserting piping and stitch. Trim the allowance to about 5 mm, notch the curves and trim the corners. Join the back section in the same way (fig 5).

If you do not want to make a gusset you could trim the foam with scissors to make a smooth curve at the top so that the front and back sections can be joined to each other.

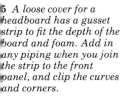

5 A loose cover for a headboard has a gusset strip to fit the depth of the board and foam. Add in any piping when you join the strip to the front panel, and clip the curves and corners.

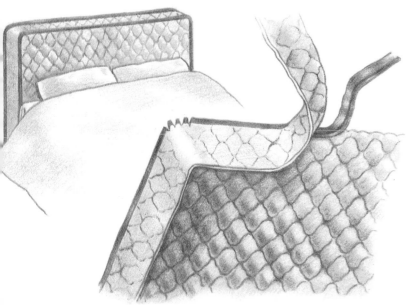

Along the open bottom end of the cover, turn up a double 6 mm hem. Add tapes for tying the cover under the board at intervals of about 30 cm to prevent it slipping around in use.

Wall-fixed bedhead

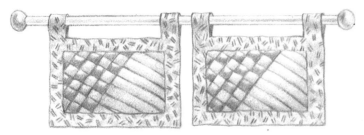

1 *Tightly stuffed welted cushions can be hung by tabs from a pole. Work any decorative features before you make up the cushions.*

A completely different approach to furnishing the head end of the bed consists of attaching a cushion or a pair of box cushions to the wall, a particularly elegant arrangement if hung from a brass or wooden rod, as in fig 1. The cushions should hang to a point just above the top of the mattress, and can be as high as is convenient. Make sure that the pole is high enough up the wall so you do not bang your head against it. The cushions should be stuffed with layers of wadding, perhaps in terylene or upholsterer's felt (linter's felt). Feathers or loose filling are not suitable because they will fall to the bottom of the cushion. Make the cushion into a pad, as thin as you wish, providing there is enough stuffing or padding in it so that you cannot feel the wall through it. Continue making the box cushions as described on page 97. Make the loops that will attach the cushions to the rod. Each loop will probably be about 40 cm long and 10 cm wide, but remember when cutting them out to allow for seam turnings. Follow the method for making curtain tabs (page 34). Sew the loops into the cushion casing to either side of the top gusset.

You can of course develop this idea by sewing decorative patterns on to the cushion front, or by making them up from quilting (see page 136).

Bed hangings

If you have a four-poster bed you may want to give it elaborate treatment with a frilled bedspread or valance but you will have to divide the cover and the frill at the bottom corners because of the posts (see page 53). You may also want to make up a valance (or frill) to run round the top, or drapes round the posts, or even a fabric canopy to cover the roof.

All valances designed to hang round the top of a bed must be lined because they are seen from both sides. You should decide whether to line them in the same or in a contrasting fabric. You can bind either or both edges with contrasting bias binding. There are two methods of hanging the valances: either by sewing a casing through which the poles can be slotted, or, if the poles are not detachable, by affixing a standard curtain tape (the same used for curtains – page 17).

Valance with a cased heading

Decide on the depth of the valance (probably about 30 cm) and add on the circumference of the pole and 2.5 cm for turnings. Cut four strips of the main fabric all of this depth, two $1\frac{1}{2}$ to 2 times the length of the side poles and two $1\frac{1}{2}$ to 2 times the length of the end poles. Cut four equivalent lining strips. Make up the four valances separately by attaching the main fabric to the lining, right sides together, along the sides and bottom edge. Trim the corners, turn and press. Press in the top edges to the lining side by a centimetre or so, then turn them down again to a depth that will contain the pole snugly but without difficulty when the frill is ruched up. Tack along this line and then machine-stitch close to the lower edge of the casing. The pole can now be inserted into the casing (fig 2).

If you want to have a small frill at the top of the casing, add on an extra centimetre to the depth

of the four strips. Turn in the top edges of the facing fabric and the lining so that the raw edges are hidden between them and slipstitch them together. Make two lines of stitching for the casing, the top one four or five centimetres down from the top, the other beneath it leaving enough room for the pole to slip in easily (fig 3).

Valance with curtain tape

Measure the length of the valances as for those with a cased heading but add 7.5 cm for the top frill. Proceed as if you were making lined curtains (see page 18). The finished valances can be hung by ordinary curtain hooks, or attached to curtain rings or screw eyes the length of the frame.

Canopies

Even more exotic or romantic hangings can be achieved with a canopy over the bed. The canopy is really a roof covering the whole of the bed and can be plain or ruched.

Make up four lined valances, joining the bottom and the sides. Make two rows of gathering along the top edges 2 and 2.5 cm from the edge. Cut two pieces of fabric for the canopy the size of the rectangle formed by the poles plus 5 cm added to the length and width to allow for turnings. The upper piece may be lining fabric as it will not be seen.

Attach the four valances to the canopy, with the lining side of the valance to the right side of the lower canopy, raw edges level. The gathers

2 Plain casing for a valance. Turn down the top into a narrow hem, then fold that down to form a casing wide enough to contain the pole comfortably. Machine-stitch along the lower edge.

3 Frilled casing. The front fabric and lining are slipstitched together at the top. Make a casing for the pole a short distance below the top.

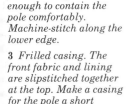

2

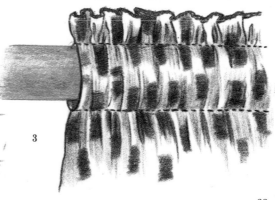

3

1 *Attach the four separate valances to the canopy, lined side of valance to right side of the lower canopy, raw edges level. The gathers should be evenly spaced all the way round.*

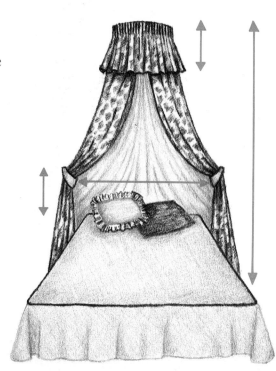

2 *The critical measurements for a corona and drapes. Use an old sheet to help you get the proportions right before you measure.*

should be evenly spaced and the end kept within the seam allowances (fig 1). Press the seam towards the canopy.

Press 2.5 cm in all round the top piece of the canopy, forming mitres at the corners. Tack the corners. Pin the two canopy sections together, wrong sides together, so that all the turnings are enclosed. Topstitch all round close to the edge.

For a *ruched canopy*, cut the lower rectangle to 1½ times the length of the finished length. Gather down the sides before joining it to the valances.

Corona and drapes

If you have an ordinary bed but want to achieve a luxurious effect, one solution may be a corona bedhead with drapery. A substantial amount of fabric is involved so you could consider making the drapery in net which would create a lighter, softer effect at less expense than if you used a heavier fabric.

When coronas were in widespread use it was normal to make both the bedhead and the bedspread in the same fabric as the corona, giving a rich and luxurious impression, but you may feel that contrasting fabrics would be just as effective.

The corona consists of a backcloth behind the bedhead and two side curtains joined to it, held back from the bed by being draped over ornamental projections called ombres. Fabric tie-backs attached to ornamental wall hooks or rings are easy to make and would be equally attractive (see page 32). The curtains and backcloth are hung from an overhead projection – the corona itself – which is trimmed with a pelmet to hide the curtain rail. It used to be the practice to buy a metal corona with all the fittings attached. They are still available occasionally from specialist hardware retailers but you could make one yourself and improvise the necessary fittings.

Planning the corona and drapery is important

so study pictures and examples and make a scale drawing in order to get the proportions right (fig 2). A corona is usually about 240 cm from the floor. The ombres or other fixtures should be about 15 cm higher than the top of the bed, and between 30 cm and 40 cm out from the sides, but experiment with a sheet to see what will suit your bed best.

The length of the backcloth will be the height of the corona to the floor. Its width will be the width between the draping points. Allow twice the fullness of fabric. The backcloth is generally left unlined.

To measure for the side curtains, drape a tape in a graceful curve from the centre front of the corona, down to where the curtains will be tied back, and then straight to the floor. Add a total of 7.5 cm for top turnings and hem. A 120 cm width is adequate for each curtain. Remember to buy enough for two curtains. They may be lined with the same fabric, or curtain lining or net.

Also remember to buy enough fabric and lining for the corona and its fabric pelmet, and for the tie-backs if they are to be in the same fabric. The pelmet depth is normally about an eighth of the total drop. Measure round the curved edge and make up widths of fabric to about double that measurement to allow for fullness.

To make your own corona, prepare a half-circle of plywood (5-ply is best). The measurement is flexible but a good-sized one for a double bed would be about 80 cm along the straight back edge, and 22 cm in depth from the back. For a single bed version, 50 cm along the back extending to 22 cm at the front of the curve would be about right.

The underside of the corona must be covered. Use the plywood as a pattern, cutting the fabric a little larger so that you can turn under the raw edges. Screw in half a dozen small hook eyes, at intervals of 6 or 7 cm, just in from the edge of the corona's curve, and a few along the back straight

edge. Remove them, glue the turned-in fabric in place, and refit them into the same holes through the fabric.

Make a pelmet as described on page 23, long enough to go round the curve from wall to wall. Pin it to the top of the board, or tack it round the front edge with tacks under the trimming. Fit the board to the wall with a couple of strong bookshelf brackets.

Make up the side curtains as for normal curtains with attached linings (see page 20), except that the tape should be sewn on to the right side of the fabric – otherwise you will be looking up at the working fixtures of the curtain as you lie in bed. The lining or self-lining should be lockstitched to the curtain (see page 21).

Lightly chalk out the shape of the backcloth on the floor, marking the pelmet width, the width between draping points at the sides of the bed, and the relevant lengths. Now drape the backcloth fabric on the floor, drawing it up to accommodate the fullness. Trim away the excess fabric equally on both sides. Turn up a double hem at the bottom and sides and fit a curtain tape to the top on the wrong side.

Slipstitch the side curtains to the backcloth fabric. Sew tapes on the wrong side of the side curtains for fixing to the ombres, or else make tie-backs (see page 32).

Hang the backcloth to the hook eyes along the back of the corona, and the side curtains round the curve of the pelmet. Overlap the two front edges.

Drape the fabric gracefully over the ombres at the shoulders of the bed and tie them with the tapes, or fit up the drapery with the tie-backs.

There are a number of variations you could consider. You might dispense with the backcloth, hang the side curtains from a pole fixed to the ceiling (through a ceiling joist) at right angles to the wall, give the curtains frilled edges, or trim them and the pelmet with fringing or braid.

Dressing-table cover

You may have a kidney-shaped dressing-table which is the traditional style for this cover with its skirt and short valance, but any small chest-of-drawers, table or even basin unit can be treated similarly in order to bring it into your bedroom or bathroom's decorating scheme.

Most kidney-shaped dressing-tables have a piece of protective glass cut to the shape of the top surface, but if yours is without glass you should be prepared to wash it often. A cotton/polyester mix would therefore be a good choice, or you could make the skirt in an easy-care cotton with the top and valance cut from matching quilted fabric. You will need to pad and/or stiffen the top if you don't use quilted fabric. Hand quilting or patchwork could be worked into the valance (see page 26) or embroidery or appliqué work. Also consider piping round the top edge.

If you would prefer a piece of glass, make a paper pattern by tracing round the top of the kidney shape, and ask your glazier to cut and grind the edge of a piece of glass to size.

For the skirt curtains you will need 1½ times the circumference of the top of the piece of furniture, whatever the shape. Divide that figure by the width of the material on the roll to find out how many widths you will need. The depth of the skirt will be from the curtain track to 1 cm above the floor, plus a total of 10 cm for heading and hem. Multiply that depth by the number of widths needed for the curtains to arrive at how much fabric to buy.

The valance will need the same width of fabric to a depth of about 15 cm; allow about 5 cm on top of that for the seam allowance and the hem.

The top can probably be cut from one width of fabric – measure the dressing-table from front to back, and add this on to your requirements.

A feature peculiar to the kidney-shaped dressing-table is its overhanging top which allows room to attach a curtain track. You will have to fix an overhanging top to any furniture that does not allow for curtain track space. If there are no drawers, such as below a basin unit, easy access to the area behind the curtains is less important, so you could dispense with the track and hang the curtains on a plastic-coated wire. Adapt the principle outlined on page 29 – the wire should grip the sides of the unit so that the curtains don't dip. Buy curtain track to fit round the dressing-table allowing for a centre-front overlap of about 3 cm – more will hinder access to the drawers. Fix the track to the underside of the overhang.

Make up and hang the curtains in the usual way (see page 17). The only opening will be at the centre front. You could enclose the edges with contrasting binding as an alternative to taking the hems up normally.

To make the top, cut a pattern from brown paper to the exact size of the surface. From the pattern cut out the fabric (and wadding and lining if necessary) allowing an extra 2.5 cm all round for seams. Pin the fabric, wadding and lining together and tack all round the seam line. Sew on piping if you are using it (see page 80) – clip into the seam allowances to enable the piping to curve properly.

Make up the valance, again binding the hem if you like, but don't finish the top edge. Instead, gather it up and pin it round the top piece, clipping into the seam allowance. Neaten the seams by hand overcasting or machine zigzagging.

Waste-paper bin cover

A simple operation can transform an otherwise ordinary waste-paper bin into an attractive and matching accessory for your room. Any odd rectangle of fabric will do the job, but you may want it to match the curtains or bed cover. Apply Scotchguard to it as protection against scuffs.

Measure the height and the circumference of the bin. (If the bin is conical, measure the circumference of the top edge rather than the base.) This will give you the width and length of the cover. Add on 2.5 cm for turnings to each dimension. Cut out the fabric, and wrap it round the bin. Turn in the raw edge, and slip-stitch the outer fold in place.

If there is any 'spring' in the fabric, mark with dressmaker's chalk where the seam is to be. Then machine-sew the seam, right sides together, and pull the tube over the bin. Fold up the bottom hem and glue it in place flush with the floor. Follow the same procedure for the top.

For decoration, glue braid round the top edge. You could glue braid round the bottom edge also – it will balance well if it is slightly wider than the one used to trim the top. You could also conceal the vertical seam with a length of braid.

Loose covers and cushions

However finely made and attractive your upholstered furniture is when new, it gradually becomes worn and soiled through daily use. Many Victorian house-holders had a sensible approach to the problem. Most pieces of furniture were bought to last a lifetime and so were carefully maintained over the years with layers of covers. Over good quality upholstery they fitted a loose cover in an attractive fabric, and over that in turn they tied a cheap cover, almost a dust sheet. This top cover was acceptable for everyday use by the family. If visitors were due, the top covers came off, revealing the loose cover underneath. If the visitors were important enough, the loose cover also came off, to reveal the upholstered furniture in its unblemished glory. Astute visitors could judge their standing in the eyes of the host from the way the furniture was uncovered.

There are better reasons for having loose covers than to make obtuse comments on guests' social standing. Apart from keeping the furniture in good condition, the loose cover can be made in a quite different fabric, so that you can change the appear-ance and character of a room in a few minutes. As the cover gets dirtier in everyday wear, you simply take it off and wash it or have it dry-cleaned.

Instead of hoping to protect a new piece of furniture you may want to cover an old chair or sofa. First make sure that the basic structure is solid and that the existing cover is clean. Vacuum the chair including down the crevices and underneath, and shampoo and mothproof it if necessary. Check the casters before

you measure for the fabric as the height of the chair may be affected if you have to change them.

Loose covers are not suitable for covering leather, plastic or wicker-work chairs; a velvet base is no good either because the pile sets up a resistance which prevents the loose cover from lying correctly. The fabric should not be too thick as at many points in the construction several layers have to be sewn together, especially where piping is involved. Plain fabric tends to show spots, sewing errors and creases. Slubbed and loose-woven materials are not suitable and dress-making fabrics are unlikely to be hard-wearing enough. Fabric with a large pattern is uneconomical because you have to centre the main motifs, and in any case the apparently bold effect when seen on the roll may be lost on a small chair.

The ideal fabric to choose therefore is one that is hard-wearing, pre-shrunk, fade- and crease-resistant, of good quality and with a fairly small pattern which will allow for the most economical cutting and which won't show spots or minor mistakes. Linen union, damask, heavy cotton or a not-too-thick repp are usual choices.

Loose covers are bulky so you may only ever want to dry-clean them, but if you do plan to wash them (perhaps in the large machine at the laundrette), ask the shop assistant's advice about shrinkage. If you wash the cover, fit it back on the chair when it is still slightly damp so that if any shrinkage has occurred the cover can stretch back to its proper size. Iron it on the chair.

Armchair cover 70

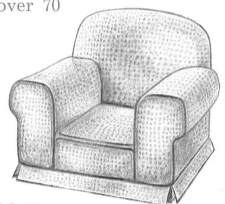

Cushions 92

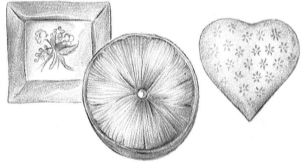

Pouffe 100

Stool 102

Canvas chairs 102

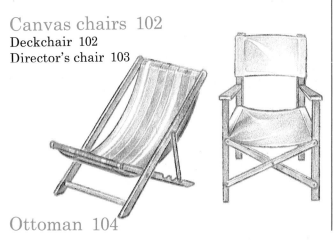

Ottoman 104

Armchair cover

Tools and materials

Apart from the fabric, you will need a fabric tape measure, tacking cotton, ordinary cotton thread (two or three reels per chair) in the predominant colour of the fabric, medium-weight piping cord (probably grade 2 or 3), a 30–45 cm zip or length of Velcro (see page 84), or hooks and eyes (size 0), sharp cutting-out scissors, steel pins (preferably with glass heads), a piping or zipper foot for the sewing-machine (it is not feasible to consider sewing a loose cover by hand), a packet of suitable sewing-machine needles, dressmaker's chalk, graph paper and an iron. Upholstery skewers would also be a help if you happen to have some already.

Measuring the chair

An average chair takes 7 m of fabric or five times the height of the back of the chair. You should use this only as a figure for costing the project. Accurate measurement is essential to establish the actual length of fabric to buy. You may find it helpful to draw a chart of the chair parts, marking in the dimensions.

The main project described here is a relatively simple design for a straightforward armchair. It has piping round the outside back, along the outer arm, and round the arm front. There is also a skirt (or valance) in three variations, all with piping running along the top. Later in the section are instructions for other styles of chairs, and adaptations for a sofa cover are given. Cushion covers are described on page 97.

The cutting list is as follows:

Inside back	(× 1)
Seat	(× 1)
Front border	(× 1)
Inside arm	(× 2)
Outside arm	(× 2)
Front arm panel	(× 2)
Outside back	(× 1)
Skirt	(optional – see below)

Write down the list, with any additional parts your chair might have, such as wings or seat cushions (see page 97) and add the measurements to the cutting list. Use a fabric tape measure to establish the chair's dimensions. The measurements will all be rectangles to facilitate the cutting out – the pieces will be trimmed to the correct shape at the fitting stage.

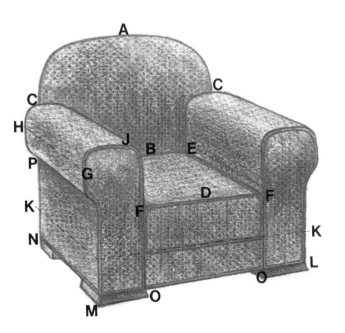

Inside back   Measure from the top rear edge of the chair down to the point where the inside back meets the seat (**A–B**). Add 15 cm for a tuck-away. Add a total of 5 cm for the two seams at the top and bottom. The tuck-away is a generous allowance of fabric which you push down between the seat and back, and between the seat and arms, when you have sewn the whole cover together. It is designed to give you some latitude in fitting the cover to the chair, and you will find that you can smooth the finished cover into a good fit by pushing and adjusting the tuck-away. It also helps to hold the cover in place without it creasing.

Measure the width of the inside back at its widest point and add 5 cm for the seams (2.5 cm at each side).

Seat   Measure from the point where the seat meets the inside back, to the peak of the middle of the front edge (**B–D**). Add 15 cm for the tuck-away at the back, and a total of 5 cm for the seams. Measure across the seat at the widest point to where the seat meets the inside arms (either **E–E** or **F–F**). Add 30 cm to give a 15 cm tuck-away at each side, and a further 5 cm for the side seams (2.5 cm at each side).

Inside arm   First determine the line along the top outer curve of the arms (**G–H**), where the inside and outside arms will meet. The design of the chair may dictate the position. In most loose covers, this line is defined by a length of piping, and because it is conspicuous it needs to be well balanced. Mark along it with several pins if it is not obvious. Measure the height of the inside arm from the point where it meets the seat, to the line you have marked (**F–G**). Add 15 cm for the tuck-away. Add a further 5 cm for 2.5 cm seams at top and bottom.

Measure the length of the line from where the top of the arm meets the front panel of the arm (**J**), to where the inside and outside back meet near the top of the arm (**C**). This will give you the longest dimension for the inside arm piece. If you measure it at any other point you may cut it too short. Add 5 cm for the two 2.5 cm seams. Allow for two inside arms.

Outside arm   This is the first stage at which you should consider fitting a skirt. The skirt is not essential but it does give a good finish to any chair or sofa which is upholstered to floor level. It is not appropriate on some kinds of chair, for example a winged chair with curvy carved legs.

First settle the height of the skirt: 12–15 cm will probably be about right. To give an ample working margin, measure for the outside arm from a position 8–10 cm above the floor, to the pinned line at the top of the outside arm (**K–H**). Add 2.5 cm for the seam at the top. If you are not going to have a skirt, measure right down to the floor.

Measure the width of the outside arm from the edge of the front arm panel to the outside back (**G–H**). Add 2.5 cm for each seam at the front and back. Allow for two of these parts.

Front arm panels   If there is to be a skirt it will meet the bottom of these panels, so measure the height from the top of the arm (**J**) to your point 8–10 cm above the floor (or else down to the floor). Add a generous 5 cm for two seams. Measure the width across the panel from the inside arm to the outside arm at the widest point. There will be two of these pieces.

Front border   Again, if you are making a skirt it will cover the bottom of this piece, so measure from the front edge of the seat (**D**) down to your line 8–10 cm from the floor. Add 2.5 cm for that seam. Otherwise, measure down to the floor. Measure the width from the inside arm at one side to the inside arm at the other (**F–F**), and a total of 5 cm for the two seams. Allow for just one piece.

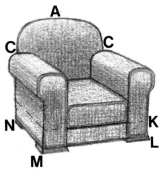

Outside back Measure from the top of the back (**A**) to the floor or skirt line (8–10 cm from the floor), and across the back at its widest point. Note that many chairs have a bulge where the arms meet the back. Take this into account to avoid being short of material at a later stage. Add 5 cm to both height and width for the seams. There will be one piece only to these dimensions.

Skirt The precise measurement of the skirt depends on the style you choose for it. For a corner kick-pleat skirt you will need one width of fabric for each side, plus one for the front and one for the back – four widths altogether. Add 5 cm to each length for turnings. The depth will be 12–15 cm plus 5 cm for a double hem at the bottom, plus 2.5 cm for the seam at the top (19.5 cm–22.5 cm). You will also need three rectangles of fabric for the backs of the pleats, each the depth of the side panels and 30 cm wide, and two half-pleats for the back opening of the same depth and 20 cm wide.

For a frilled or flounced skirt, you will need four pieces, two double the length of **LM**, and two double the length of **MN**. A less generous frill can be achieved with pieces 1½ times the length of each side. The joins will occur at the four corners.

For box pleats you will need to join strips of fabric to a length that is three times the total length round the bottom of the chair, plus about 10 cm for the side hems. The depth of the strips will be about 20 cm (see above). You will probably be able to cut the strips from surplus fabric but remember that the pattern must run vertically on all of them.

A plain hem suitable for big boxy chairs or for wing chairs is achieved by carrying the front, back and side panels down to the base of the chair and then tying them underneath. Allow enough fabric to make four strips each 10 cm by the measurement between the legs.

Arm caps will extend the life of the loose cover since the tops of the arms get more wear than anywhere else. Allow half a metre extra for each arm cap.

Piping Piping gives style and strength to the chair cover. If you plan to make it in a contrasting fabric to the main cover, calculate your cutting requirements separately. Otherwise add piping to your main list. As a rough guide, a panel the size of the chair seat should provide enough material to cover piping. You may be able to get some of the material out of the leftover pieces from the main cutting scheme. Refer to page 80 for the details of how to cut and sew piping. Remember that it should always be cut on the bias (diagonally to the selvedge) to give flexibility in use.

Estimating the fabric

You now have all the necessary measurements. One of the easiest ways to work out how much fabric to buy is to mark out with chalk an area on the floor the width of the chosen fabric, probably 120 cm or 130 cm. Cut out rectangular pieces of newspaper to correspond to all the cover's sections (don't forget the cushion if you are planning to make one), label them and lay them within the chalked confines in the most economical way you can find, making sure that all the lengths run parallel to the edges.

If the fabric has a large pattern with central motifs, chalk off on the floor the length of the pattern repeat and the approximate position of the motif, so that you can place the focal points of the loose cover accordingly. (Remember that the motif for the centre inside back will be nearer the top of the rectangle as the bottom 15 cm of the piece will form the tuck-away.) See opposite for a typical layout plan.

Decide whether there will be enough fabric left over down the sides for the piping or whether you will need to add on to the end a panel the size

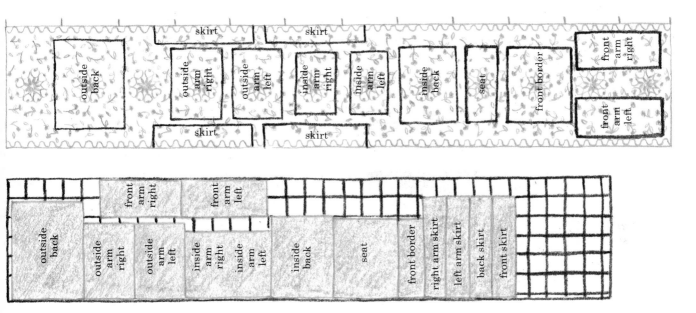

Using a large expanse of floor, or graph paper scaled down, arrange as economically as possible the rectangles of newspaper representing the parts of the cover. Label each one carefully. All lengths must run parallel to the edge of the fabric.

If the fabric has a pattern to be matched, mark the length of the pattern repeat on the floor or graph paper so that you can arrange the motifs centrally.

of the chair seat (as explained above). When you have found the best arrangement, measure the total length of the chalked area – this will be the amount of fabric to buy.

An alternative method for estimating the required amount of fabric is to make a scale drawing on graph paper, with one small square representing 10 mm, say. Cut a length of graph paper the scaled-down width of the fabric and cut similarly scaled-down rectangles to represent the various sections to lay on top of it. Mark the positions of central motifs. Don't forget to label everything.

Whichever estimating method you use, keep a record of the sequence you have arranged the pieces in so that you can refer to it when cutting out the fabric. It is best to round up your total measurement to a full metre unless you are very confident of the accuracy of your scheme.

When you have bought your fabric you should go through the measuring process again as you cut each piece. One mis-measurement could ruin the whole operation so it is worth spending extra time at this stage.

Cutting out

For cutting, refer to the sequence you devised when estimating how much fabric to buy. Lay or pin each piece in its position on the chair as you go, or set them to one side, but whichever you do, be sure to label everything – it is very easy to get muddled as you become surrounded in a sea of fabric. You will also find it helpful to mark the top, bottom and straight grain on each piece.

Cut simple rectangles at this stage – you will be trimming them to the exact shapes of the parts at the fitting stage.

Fitting the cover

1

1 Pin the inside back to the chair, right side out. Make small darts towards the sides to take up the excess fabric.

Now you can start to fit the pieces in place. The first stage is to pin them all together with both the right side of the fabric and the pinned seams facing you. At a later stage you will be turning all the seams into the inside, but if you pin carefully now you won't have to tack all the sections together later.

Lay the inside back in position and secure it with pins or upholstery skewers. On this style of cover, in which the inside back meets the outside back, you may have to form a dart or at least ease the excess fabric by gathering it up at the corners. This will be unnecessary on a chair which has a separate panel or border across the top of the back.

Draw the excess fabric up into a fold at right angles to the edge of the chair back. Push in a line of pins snugly against the upholstery of the chair to mark where the dart will be sewn (fig 1). If there is a lot of surplus fabric it would be better to make several small darts. When you come to pin the outside back to the inside back later on you will be able to check the size and positioning of the darts.

Next lay the rectangle cut for the seat in its place. Make sure that it is centrally positioned with a 2.5 cm overhang at the front, and push a couple of pins or skewers through it to hold it temporarily. At the rear of the seat, you will have a 15 cm tuck-away to match the tuck-away of the inside back. Smooth out both of these, and pin them together 2.5 cm from the edges. If they do not match, trim off the excess from the longer piece. This operation does not have to be too precise because the fabric will be pushed down inside the body of the chair.

Take up the two pieces for the inside arms and lay them in place. If there is a pattern on your fabric, the pieces should of course be mirror images of each other. Make sure the pattern is upright and even if there is no pattern, ensure that the grain of the fabric runs vertically. Push pins or upholstery skewers through the fabric into the chair to hold the material temporarily. At the bottom, there will be a tuck-away. Pin it to the seat tuck-away, just as you pinned the seat and inside back tuck-aways together. At the top, the fabric will follow the line of the chair arm and extend beyond the piping line or the line you marked earlier with pins. If the chair arm tapers, there will be an excess of material at the narrower end, so trim this off a few centimetres outside the piping line to give clearer access to your work. At the front, the fabric should extend 2.5 cm beyond the line of the chair arm. Check that it does, and insert a couple of pins to hold it in place.

Now deal with the rear part of the inside arms. This will be the first area that offers any complications. There are already two tuck-away

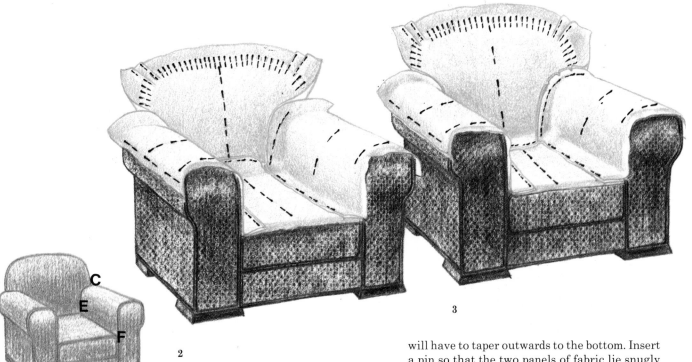

2

3

2 *Pin the inside arm to the back, starting at the bottom.*

3 *The pins taper in towards the chair as the recess becomes shallower, eventually lying snugly against the chair from the point where the recess ends. You may have to snip into the seam turnings to ease tension at the top of the curve.*

pieces (the inside back and the seat) pinned together to form a seam. There are also to be tuck-aways to the inside arms, both along the side of the seat (**FE**), and up the first few inches of the gap between the chair back and the inside arm (**EC**).

Pin the inside arm tuck-away to the seat tuck-away, starting at the rear of the seat. Pin along a line 2.5 cm in from the two edges to give a sewing line. Now draw the three pieces of the fabric together, and start pinning vertically up the seam between the inside arm tuck-away and the inside back tuck-away (fig 2).

Feel inside the uncovered chair to establish where the recess ends between the back and the arm. From here upwards there will be no tuck-away, and from here downwards the tuck-away

will have to taper outwards to the bottom. Insert a pin so that the two panels of fabric lie snugly against the chair. Working down the seam, make a neat line in pins from that point to the point where the three sections of fabric join at the bottom. Above that point, put in another line of pins to follow the line between the chair back and the chair arm (fig 3). You will find that the fabric resists following the line of the curve, so snip into the seam turnings as often as is necessary to ease the tension, but not further in than the line of pins.

Do not expect to get a perfect fit first time at this part of the project. You will probably have to re-pin the work several times until you get a satisfactory fit with a neat seam close against the upper part of the chair arm merging into an increasing quantity of tuck-away in the recess. Repeat the procedure for the other inside arm.

You can now fit the outside arms. If there is a pronounced slope in the design of the arm of the

75

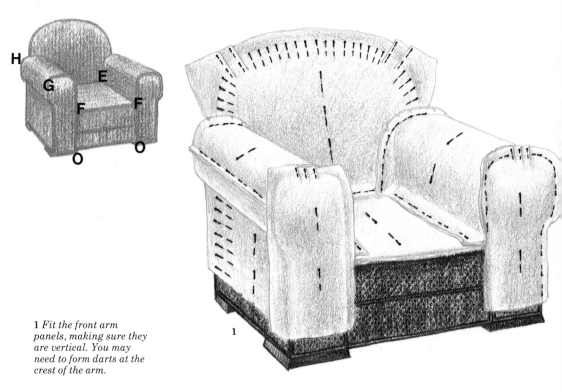

1 *Fit the front arm panels, making sure they are vertical. You may need to form darts at the crest of the arm.*

chair you will have plenty of fabric to spare. Make sure, however, that you fit this piece upright with any large motifs centrally positioned. There should be 2.5 cm seam allowances at the front and back of the chair. Position the fabric so that it extends below the line of the skirt or, if there is to be a tie-under, so that it brushes the floor. Pin the fabric in place to meet the piping line at the top (**GH**), and trim off the excess to give a 2.5 cm seam allowance.

You can now merge the inside and outside arms into a good join. Check that your piping line (**GH**) is well placed and follows a smooth straight line along the outer top part of the chair arm. Draw the two seam allowances together, and pin them as close to the arm as you

comfortably can without straining the fabric. Fit the outside arm on the opposite side.

Now fit the arm front panels (fig 1). Push four or five pins or upholstery skewers through each panel to keep it in position. Make sure that any pattern is vertical, and that the two panels are mirror images of each other. Each one should overlap the outer edge of the chair arm by 2.5 cm all round, and hang down generously below the line of the skirt.

Pin all round the panels, forming a seam between the arm front and the inside and outside arm pieces. There will eventually be piping round this line, so make sure that the seam falls exactly on the crest of the arm – otherwise the piping will droop down the arm front or drag

2 & 3 *Pin the seat border to the seat and front arm panels. The tuck-away down the side of the seat has to be pinned to fit the recess.*

back along the arm top. You may have to make a few tiny darts round the crest (fig 1).

Make a neat join at **G** where the arm front meets the seam of the inside and outside arms. Trim off any excess to give a tidy seam all round.

The seat border comes next. Pin it in place with the pattern or the grain of the fabric running vertically. Pin the seam allowance at the top to the seam allowance of the seat itself, exactly on the crown of the curve (**FF**). Pin the seam allowance at each side to the seam allowance on the arm fronts (**OF**).

You will find that these three parts – arm front, seat, and seat border – all meet at or near **F**. If you push your hand down into the recess along the side of the seat (**FE**), you can establish how

far down you can take the corresponding recess in your loose cover. Mark the position on the front arm panel with a pin. Push the tuck-away ends of the inside arm and the seat down into the gap – you pinned them together earlier but now check that the tuck-away is tapered from front to back to fit the recess. Pin round the seam between the seat and the seat border, and along the seam between the inside arm and the front arm panel. When you reach the point you have marked with a pin to show the depth of the gap, start pinning together the seat border and the arm panel, right to the bottom of those pieces of fabric (figs 2 & 3).

Repeat the operation at the other side of the seat border.

1 Fold the fabric in half to find its centre.

2 Pin it to the chair cover along the fold line, then pin round the edge of the chair. Mark where the opening is to start.

1

2

Pick up the seam allowance of the inside back along the top of the chair, and the seam allowance of the outside back, and pin the two together along the line of the crest of the chair back (**CAC**). This line will have piping, so position it as accurately as possible. Readjust any darts pinned in the inside back if necessary.

For fitting the outside back you may find it helps to tip the chair forward on to its arm fronts. Ensure that the fabric is exactly centred if there is any kind of pattern in it. To do this, measure to find the centre of the chair back and mark it with pins or chalk at top and bottom. Find the centre of the fabric by folding it, and line it up with the pins or chalk marks (fig 1). Pin the fabric in place so that there is a 2.5 cm seam allowance at the top. It should reach to just below the level of the skirt (or brush the floor if you are having a simple hem).

As you take your line of pins down the side of the chair, you will arrive at the area where three or even four parts of the loose cover meet: inside arm, outside arm, inside back, and outside back. They come together at **C** where the chair arm meets the chair back, where there may anyway be a pronounced bulge. Forming neat seams here can be tricky. If the turnings of one seam overlap those of another, fold them down together to avoid excessive bulging. If the outside back seam is unwilling to turn round any curves, snip it to ease the tension. Continue pinning down the

3 Mark round the skirt line with chalk or pins. Insert a pin close to the side of every seam to ensure accuracy later.

right side as far as the hem or the top of the skirt.

Fit this part of the work snugly but not too tight, or else it will strain the fastening at the opposite side of the back should any shrinkage occur later. In any case, loose covers are not meant to be as perfectly fitted as tacked-on upholstery covers so there is some latitude, and a slight fullness is preferable to a pulled, strained appearance.

Some arrangement has to be made for putting on the cover, fixing it in place, and removing it from time to time for washing or cleaning. The choice is between a zip, Velcro and hooks and eyes. The opening can be at either side, though to have it at the left is more usual.

Mark the point at which the fastening will begin (fig 2). As a rough guide the opening will be 30–45 cm long. On the type of chair illustrated, the correct point is 6–8 cm down from **P**. On a balloon-backed chair the fastening should close to the widest point on the back. Mark the top of the opening with pins or dressmaker's chalk, and draw the seams together. Pin them temporarily.

Go round all the seams again to check that the pinned seams are as well-fitting as possible.

Marking the seams

Mark all the seams on the cover for sewing by going right round the chair and trimming all the seam turnings so that they are an exact 2.5 cm on both pieces of fabric. Then, at intervals of 8–10 cm, cut a notch into the seam turnings through both pieces of fabric at the same time. Make the notches between a half and one centimetre deep, and roughly triangular in shape. Cut them at slightly irregular intervals in slightly different shapes and sizes so that when you are trying to sew an apparently shapeless bundle of fabric on which the seams appear to bear no relation to each other, you can line up the corresponding notches.

Now mark the line of the skirt. With a small ruler, go right round the chair and push in pins at exactly the point the skirt will be sewn to, at intervals of 10–12 cm. The skirt should eventually clear the floor by about half a centimetre so add this clearance to your measurement – say 12.5 cm for a 12 cm skirt. A conventional school ruler will do this for you: the small margin at the end before the measuring scale begins gives just about the right clearance, so you can insert pins against the 12 cm mark on the scale. Take care to insert a pin close to each side of every seam so that you will get absolute accuracy at these critical points.

Alternatively, you can mark a line with dressmaker's chalk if the fabric will take it clearly. Or you can use both marking methods (fig 3).

The cover is now fully fitted (though without the skirt) and providing you sew along the marked lines you will be able to take off the cover for sewing and put it back to the same position with the exact fit repeated.

Remove all the pins which have skewered the various parts to the chair, and carefully lift the cover away. You might find it helpful to pin back the identification labels.

Making up the piping

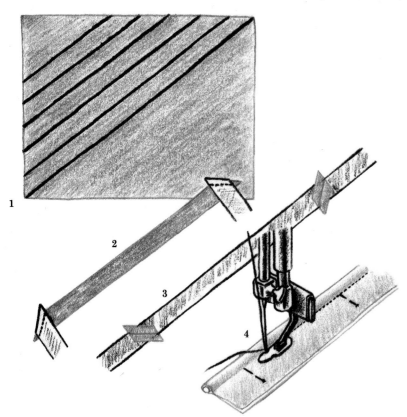

1 *Cut piping strips on the bias.*

2 & 3 *Join the strips as illustrated, snipping off the triangles that jut out beyond the finished strip.*

4 *Pin the cord inside the casing (right sides out) and machine along close to the cord.*

Before you sew the cover itself, make up your supply of piping. Piping is the thin roll which on many chairs and cushions runs along the seam lines to define them and help protect weak areas from wear.

Designers of modern upholstery sometimes dispense with piping. Others take advantage of its design potential by making it in a different fabric from the rest of the cover, so that it gives extra definition to the shape of the chair or sofa.

Piping is easy to make and consists of lengths of piping cord covered by and sewn into a long strip of fabric folded in two. Piping cord is available in thicknesses graded from 1–6. A medium grade, 2 or 3, is suitable for general use. Most suppliers stock only one grade. If you are planning to wash the loose cover rather than dry-clean it, you will need to boil the cord first as it will shrink quite badly otherwise. Pre-shrunk piping cord is available in some shops.

Mark out the fabric for your piping. In the original cutting chart you left a square available about the size of the seat, or else you decided that there would be enough surplus fabric down the sides. Cut it into strips 6 cm wide on the bias (diagonally to the selvedge). Fabric cut on the bias has more 'give' than if cut on the straight grain so is better able to follow the contours of upholstery seams. Make your first cut straight across the diagonal of the square, then further cuts on each side of it (fig 1).

Machine-sew the cut pieces into a continuous roll. Lay the first two end to end in a V-shape with the right side of one against the right side of the other. They should overlap by about 1 cm. Run them through your machine, sewing a seam about 1 cm in from the ends. The seam will run between the two angles formed at the overlapping points (fig 2).

Go straight on to the next, and sew on each section in turn to produce a continuous length. Turn it wrong side up on the ironing board and press open the seam at each join. Snip off the small triangles of excess fabric along the sides of the strip (fig 3).

Take the length back to the sewing-machine, together with the roll of piping cord. Install the piping (zipper) foot.

Fold the beginning of the strip of fabric wrong sides together and insert the length of piping cord into the end of it. Keeping the cord inside the roll well up against the piping foot, sew along the whole length (fig 4). You will produce a continuous firm roll of fabric with the cord inside it, and with two seam turnings about 2.5 cm wide. The piping is now ready to use.

Sewing the cover

In principle, the process of sewing the cover is perfectly simple. All you have to do is turn the cover inside out, turn the seams the other way, and sew along the line of pins.

In reality, of course, there are complications that can appear fearsome on the first cover you sew. You have to handle a bundle of apparently random fabric, full of pins, all of which seem to be hidden or in the wrong place. Furthermore, you will have to sew piping into some of the seams as you go. You will have to get used to identifying which part you are working on, and to turning some part of the cover inside to outside several times in the course of the operation. The idea is to work gradually round the cover inverting a seam and then sewing the re-pinned seam, including any piping, before going on to the next.

Withdraw a few pins at a time, invert the seam and re-pin it using the same holes as far as you can. As each seam becomes inverted the turnings will lie on the inside of the cover. The notches and edges should be positioned exactly as they were when you fitted the cover (fig 5).

5 *Withdraw a few pins at a time, invert the seam, and re-pin it. The edges and notches should line up exactly as before.*

Take the cover to the sewing-machine, and start to feed the re-pinned seam through it. Sew along the pin line, withdrawing each pin as it arrives at the sewing foot. If you turn and sew all your seams accurately, your cover should be the same size and shape, and therefore the same fit, as it was when you pinned the individual pieces of fabric on the chair.

Start with the darts at the top of the back. Turn them to the inside of the cover and sew them in position (you may feel more confident if you tack them first). Open each dart out on both sides of the sewing line and press it open. This will help to eliminate the ruckles which make a dart look untidy. Tie the end of the threads.

Turn next to the seam that joins the inside arm to the inside back (**CE**). This is the seam that forms a tuck-away in its lower half, fitting closely against the chair in its upper part. Continue by sewing the inside back to the seat along the tuck-away seam, and then by sewing the inside arm to the seat. Start at the rear of the seat, where two seams already meet. Form the next seam from that corner. It will follow, if you recall, the sewing line that you adjusted to meet the deepest point of the recess between the chair seat and arm. Sew along that seam, but stop sewing at a point 5 cm from the end. You will see why shortly.

The cover is now beginning to take shape, with the four main inner panels fitted in place. None of the seams for those panels has needed piping. Almost all the remaining seams on the chair *will* require piping, so re-insert the piping foot in your machine.

The first piped seams to sew are those joining the inside arm to the outside arm. There are several methods. One is to invert the seam as usual, then feed in the piping as you sew, removing the pins as each one arrives at the sewing foot. However, this involves working your piping into a narrow space between two pinned seam turnings.

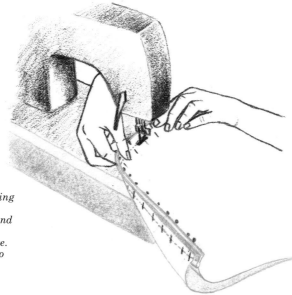

1 *One method of inserting piping is to unpin the seam, add the piping and either re-pin or tack it with the piping in place. You will then be able to sew more easily.*

One alternative – a time-consuming one but which may be the easiest in the long run – is to unpin the seam, insert the piping, and either re-pin or tack it with the piping in place. Then the sewing is easy (fig 1).

Otherwise, you might like to take a confident step forward, dispense with re-pinning, and sew the seams 'freehand'. You will find that you can bring the two seams together as they approach the sewing foot, and feed in the piping, lining up the two edges of the piping and the two edges of the seam turnings as you proceed. You must take great care to line up the notches – this may not be easy because the process of adding the piping tends to cause the lower layer of fabric to pucker slightly. The upper layer of fabric will then seem longer than the lower one. Do not be deceived into thinking that the notches were wrong – if you do so the cover will certainly fail to fit. Instead, pull and ease the fabric through the machine, and make the notches match up accurately.

Whenever you are sewing piping you will find it an advantage to arrange the work so that in any curve in the seam, the outer part of the curve is underneath. This is because the outer curve was slightly longer at the fitting stage so that even if it puckers slightly, the notches in the shorter length will still coincide.

In this case, it means putting the outside arm on the bottom, then the piping, then the inside arm on the top. (Likewise, the inside arm goes on the bottom, followed by the piping, followed by the arm front, when you come to that stage.)

Next sew the arm front panels. It is easiest to start at the bottom of the outside arm (**K**). Sew the arm front to the outside arm, with piping in the seam.

At the top of the outside arm you will encounter a junction of two piped seams (**G**). The tidiest way to deal with the bulk is to cut one length of the piping cord (but not the casing) at the point where they join. If you consider the junction as a 'T', the upright of the 'T' is the one to cut – in other words, the piping running from **G–H**. Peel back the cover of the piping as far as the sewing line of the seam which crosses the upright, cut the cord, and fold the seam down again (fig 2).

Alternatively, if your machine is strong enough, sew one piece of piping across the other piece. You can help by lifting the sewing foot and 'walking' your machine across the bulky thicknesses of fabric, turning the wheel manually.

It is best to sew the seam turnings so that they all lie in one direction, pointing towards the floor. Seam turnings which lie in a downward direction are less visible through the finished cover than those which point upwards.

From the fitting stage you will recall dealing with the gap where each side of the seat meets the arm at the front at **F**. You marked its depth with pins or dressmaker's chalk. Also, you left a 5 cm pinned seam in the tuck-away between the inside arm and seat where it neared this point.

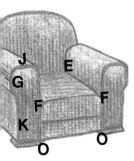

Now you will have to join together these various items – the seat and front border, the inside arm and arm front, and the remainder of that seam between the seat and inside arm. The front border and arm front must also be joined below the gap. And there will be two sets of piping, one across the front border and one down the arm front, which must merge together.

Sew the piped seam between the arm front and the inside arm down as far as the pin at **F**. Leave enough piping dangling to reach the bottom of the seam eventually. Next sew the piped seam between the seat and seat border (**F–F**). Cut off the cord (not the casing), and roll the remaining piped seam running from **J–O** over the fabric of the piping you have just cut, and continue to sew to the bottom of the new seam. Finally close the 5 cm gap between the inside arm and the seat (fig 3).

Again, you may find that with so many thicknesses of fabric at the point where the two piped seams join, an ordinary household sewing-machine cannot cope. If that is the case, raise the sewing foot and 'walk' the work through manually, or finish the seam by hand.

The most difficult part of the job is now over, and you can go on to sew the outside back to the rest of the cover. Locate the point where the zip opening starts, and with the notches accurately arranged, snip into the seams at that point. Invert the seams from there all round the chair back to the bottom on the opposite side. This seam will be piped. Sew from the skirt line (or the hem if you are not having a skirt) on the back only, with the piping in place, joining in the outer arm just below **P** at the top of the opening. Place the notches accurately throughout (fig 4).

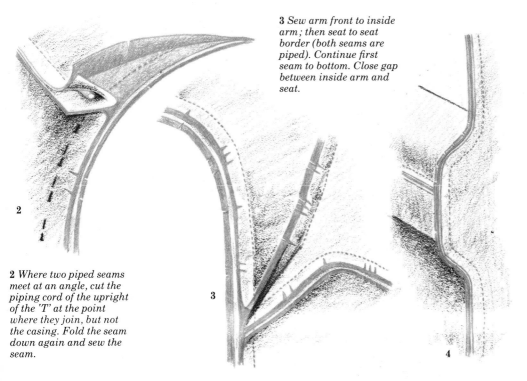

3 *Sew arm front to inside arm; then seat to seat border (both seams are piped). Continue first seam to bottom. Close gap between inside arm and seat.*

2

3

4

2 *Where two piped seams meet at an angle, cut the piping cord of the upright of the 'T' at the point where they join, but not the casing. Fold the seam down again and sew the seam.*

4 *Snip into the seam where the opening will start, matching notches above accurately. Below that point, sew piping to the back section only of the cover – do not join the outside arm.*

The opening

You will be left with an opening which you will have to fix by some method to allow you to put on and take off the cover.

The hooks and eyes method To carry the hooks and eyes, you will have to reinforce the two sides of the opening because they have to bear the strain of keeping the cover closed against some slight shrinkage in the material. Measure the length of the opening. Add 2.5 cm and cut two pieces of fabric to this length, 7.5 cm wide and on the bias of the fabric.

Pin the placket material on top of the piping along the outside back edge of the opening. Sew round the placket as in fig 1 and take it over the top where the outside back joins the outside arm.

Open out the placket and you should see the piping neatly enclosed. Fold the placket round over the raw edges to the wrong side and hem-stitch it in place. You can now sew hooks-and-eyes tape or individual hooks and eyes to the placket at intervals of 4 or 5 cm (fig 2).

Velcro Buy enough of it to fit the length of the opening and the same amount and width of cotton tape or seam binding. Sew one half of the Velcro and the tape together, wrong sides facing each other down one side. Insert the raw edge of the outside back into them and tack it in place. Pin and then sew the opposite length of Velcro to the outside arm opening, overlapping it by about 15 mm. Bring the Velcro strips together at the top of the placket, pin them and then machine across the top. Fold the second Velcro strip to the outside so that the raw edge is enclosed and hem it in place (figs 3, 4 & 5).

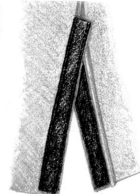

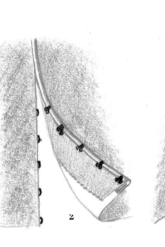

1 *Pin and sew the placket to the opening, right sides together.*

2 *Fold it round to the wrong side of the cover and hem it in place before sewing on hooks and eyes.*

3, 4 & 5 *The stages for attaching Velcro strips and tape.*

Zip To put in a zip, you will need to use the zipper or piping foot on the machine. Turn under the raw, unpiped edge and tack it in place (fig 6). Lay the closed zip under this edge, right side up and with the opening end of the zip at the bottom. Pin and tack it. Bring the piped edge over the zip and tack along the edge of the piping (figs 7 & 8). From the right side, and starting at the top, stitch down close to the cord. Open the zip. Stitch across the top of the opening and down the other side (fig 9). It is important to sew the two sides of the zip in the same direction so that the material won't pull. Trim the turnings even with the zip's tape and overcast the edges together.

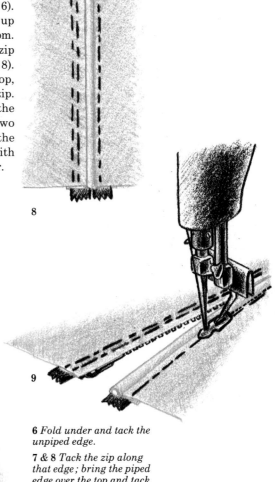

8

6

7

9

6 *Fold under and tack the unpiped edge.*

7 & 8 *Tack the zip along that edge; bring the piped edge over the top and tack it.*

9 *Stitch across the top, then down the two sides in the same direction.*

Tie-under finish

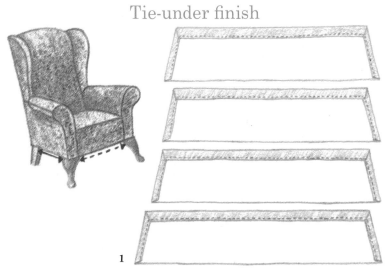

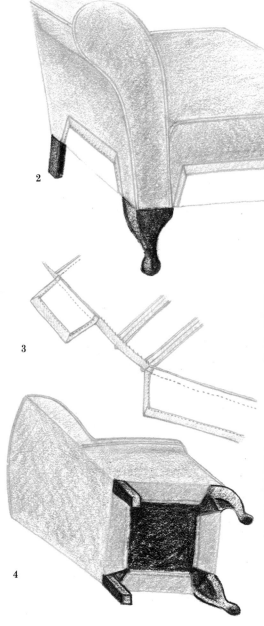

1 *Give the narrower edge of each strip a moderately wide hem to form a casing.*

2 *Stitch the casings to the bottom of the chair cover.*

3 *Make facings to neaten the corners.*

4 *Introduce tapes into the four casings to tie round the back of the legs.*

For a plain hem that will give an uncluttered, tailored look, especially suitable on chairs such as wing chairs where the legs will show, you will have allowed in your cutting plan for four strips 10 cm deep, by the measurement between each leg, plus 5 cm for hems.

Finish the cover itself and apply the fastening (zip, Velcro or hooks and eyes – see overleaf). Cut the sides of the four strips to a slight angle and hem them. The bottom hem should be slightly wider to form a casing (fig 1). Pin and then stitch the casings to the base of the cover between the legs (fig 2).

Cut a 5 cm wide facing to fit the shape of each corner, and machine it on, right sides together, about 1 cm from the edge. Turn the facing and press. Turn under a narrow hem and oversew the edge to the cover (fig 3).

Introduce a length of tape into the four casings each long enough to tie comfortably at the ends (fig 4). Four more tapes could usefully be sewn on halfway along each casing for tying centrally under the chair – this might help particularly on a large chair or sofa.

Making the skirt

If you are planning to have a skirt, you will have already determined its design in the cover's planning stages. Its correct height off the floor should be marked with a line of pins or dressmaker's chalk on the sewn cover. Regardless of the style of skirt it is easiest to sew on the piping at this stage. Sew it on to the cover, starting and finishing at the opening, so that the corded part is uppermost and the raw edges point to the floor. Make one end abut with the piping running down the back half of the opening by peeling back the casing and cutting the cord level, then tucking the end of the casing down into the seam (fig 5).

Corner pleats The simplest and most economical design of skirt, suitable for a wide range of chairs, has straight sides and inverted kick-pleats at the corners. You will already have cut four panels, two the length of the sides, and one each the length of the back and the front of the chair, plus seam turnings. Each piece should have an extra 5 cm at the bottom for a double hem, and 2.5 cm at the top for the turning. You will also have cut five pieces for the pleats.

Join all the pieces together in this order, using a flat seam, right sides together: half-pleat, left side panel, pleat, front, pleat, right side panel, pleat, back, half-pleat. Mark the vertical centre of each full pleat with dressmaker's chalk or iron in a crease. Press the seams open. Machine-sew a double 2.5 cm hem all round the bottom, and given the vertical ends of the half-pleats double 2.5 cm hems too.

Pin the strip to the rest of the cover, bringing the centres of the pleats and the ends of the skirt panels to the corners. Trim round to make a neat 2.5 cm seam allowance and cut notches at irregular intervals (fig 6).

Now gradually unpin the skirt and re-pin it as for the rest of the cover so that the seams end up on the wrong side, matching corners, edges and notches. Sew round the seam close to the piping, starting from the back left opening. Neaten the edges. Sew poppers to the edges of the half-pleats so that these form a full pleat.

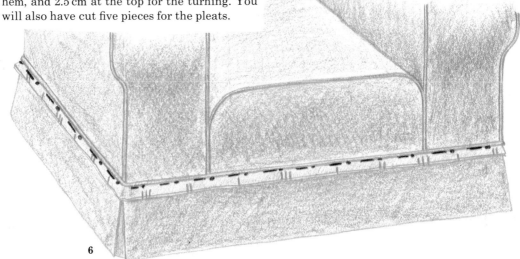

5 Sew piping to the cover before you attach the skirt.

6 Pin the skirt to the cover, cutting notches all round.

5

6

Frilled or flounced skirt Join in the correct order the four strips of material you cut out (left side, front, right side, back). Take up and machine-sew a double 2.5 cm hem, and give the vertical ends narrow double hems. Gather up each side individually with two rows of gathering threads. Then pull up each panel to fit the corresponding side of the chair and adjust the gathers, pinning as you go. Trim the seam allowance.

Invert the seam allowance as usual. This time you will have no notches to match up but the depth of the turning will be uniform. Again, readjust the gathers, tack and then sew them in position. Neaten the edges.

Box pleats The length of each pleat will be dictated by the length of each side of the chair, but will be as near as possible to 10 cm wide. Join the cut-out strips together, right sides together, and press the seams open. Take up and machine-sew a double 2.5 cm hem along the bottom edge. Starting along the left side of the chair, divide the length into equal pleats as near as possible to 10 cm wide, leaving about 3 cm clear at the beginning – this will form a placket or turning at the opening. Make a cardboard template to form accurate pleats. It should be the exact width and depth of the pleats you want. The depth will be from the skirt line down to 5 mm above the floor.

Lay the strip of material out flat, wrong side up. Using the template, mark with chalk or pins the positions of the designated number of pleats for the left side.

Then consider the front of the chair. You may have to cut another template which will enable you to achieve equal pleats ending at the corners, but it must not differ too much from the first template or else the finished effect will look uneven.

The right side will be the same as for the left side, but you may have to make a third template for the back if the chair is wider at front or back.

1 *Box pleats. Seams should be hidden at the back. Tack along the top and leave excess fabric at the ends.*

Form the pleats by bringing the pins or chalked lines together, contriving that all the seams joining the strips are hidden at the back. At the end of the back there should be more than enough fabric to turn in 3 cm to form the other side of the placket. Tack along the top of the pleats (fig 1).

Bring up the strip of box pleats to the chair cover. The pleats should lie neatly at the corners. Trim the seam allowance and cut notches at irregular intervals. Re-pin the skirt with the seam turnings to the inside, matching corners and notches. Sew round the seam next to the piping. Neaten the edges.

Arm caps

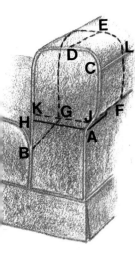

It is worth making a pair of arm caps for the loose cover since the front end of the arm suffers the worst of the wear and gets easily soiled. If you have no arm caps you will find the condition of the loose cover deteriorates rapidly, and you will have to take it off for frequent cleaning. Refer to the adjacent drawing throughout.

Most arm caps consist of a front panel ending just below the line of the scroll, or 15–20 cm down the arm front if there is no scroll. The front panel is attached to the cap which runs from the outside lower corner of the front panel on the outside arm (**A**), over the arm itself, and down to the point where the seat meets the inside arm of the chair. If there is a cushion, the arm cap should fit neatly between the cushion and the chair arm, where it will be held in place (**B**). If there is no cushion, it can be made to fit a few centimetres into the recess to hold it in place. The arm cap is piped.

Start by making a template or pattern of the front of one of the arms. Bear in mind that you will be making two arm caps, mirror images of each other. Pin a piece of stiff paper (brown paper is ideal) to the front of the arm. Mark round it the shape of the arm by rubbing it with a pencil or the back of your scissors, or by cutting into it to meet the chair, and cutting round the template between the cuts (fig 2). Mark on the template the point (**C**) where the arm piping which runs along the arm back-to-front on the arm covers meets the arm front panel.

For the other section, take three measurements. The first is from the front of the arm (**D**) to the point where you want the arm cap to end along the top of the arm (**E**). The next is from the bottom lower corner of the outside panel (**A**), up along the line of the scroll as far as **C**, which is where the inside arm meets the outside arm on the chair itself. The final measurement is from that junction (**C**), up over the top of the arm and

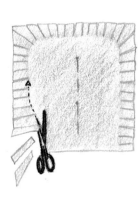

2 *Pin brown paper to the arm front. Snip into it all round, then trim off the cut parts to get a template.*

down to **B** between the cushion and the inside arm. Add 2.5 cm to every dimension where there will be a seam and 5 cm to every dimension which will end in a hem.

If you have a patterned fabric, you will have to cut the panels that meet at **CL** in such a way that when sewn the pattern on each side of the arm will be the right way up.

To cut the front panel, pin the template to your fabric (right side up). Don't forget the seam and hem allowances – these measurements are most easily marked with dressmaker's chalk.

Pin the sections together, right sides facing outwards, in the same way that you pinned the chair cover. Start by pinning together the two panels over the arm. Sew them together, adding in a length of piping. Open out the piping case at **C** and cut the end of the cord flush with the seam (don't cut the casing itself). Sew round a double 2.5 cm hem from **F** to **G**, cutting off excess piping so that the hem will lie flat.

Pin on a second length of piping to run eventually from **A** to **H** but only sew it on between **J** and **K** for the moment – in other words round from hem to hem. Leave the two ends hanging (fig 3).

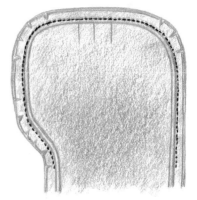

3 *Sew piping round the seam leaving free the two* ends that will be taken up in the hem.

Pin and hand-sew a double 2.5 cm hem at the bottom of the front panel (**HA**). Pin that panel to the top section with a 2.5 cm seam allowance on both pieces, right sides out, so that the piping running from **C** to **L** matches up with the marked spot on the front panel. Clip round the curves in as far as the seam line to ease the tension.

Re-pin the pieces so that the seam allowance is on the wrong side, matching up the notches where you clipped the seam. Sew round the top of the arm cap from **K** to **J**, preferably twice for increased strength.

You will be left with the two ends of piping. Hand-sew together the hems of the front and side at **KH** and **JA**, contriving to enclose the end of the piping into the fold of one hem for a neat finish. Hem the rest of the front panel between **H** and **B** which will tuck down past the cushion or into the chair's crevice.

Go on to make the other arm cap, cutting and sewing every part to make a reverse of the first one. You may want to sew on a couple of strips of Velcro near to point **E** to hold the arm caps in place. The caps will be easy to take off for cleaning and will add years of life to the main loose cover.

Wing chair cover

Follow the usual principles for measuring for any loose cover – in other words, measure at the widest points. Treat the wings as elements separate from the arms, so that you will have four rectangles for each side: inside wing, outside wing, inside arm, outside arm. The horizontal seam at the base of the wing will be a continuation of the top of the arm. The edges of the wings will be piped. Wing chairs rarely have a skirt unless their legs are very ugly, so plan for a tie-under finish (see page 86).

When you come to fit the cover, deal with the inside and outside back pieces first. Then apply the wing pieces and cut them very roughly to the finished shape. You may find it easier to make a paper pattern at this point. Pin the back wings to the outside back and the inside wings to the inside back, making sure that the seams rest snugly against the chair's contours. Pull the outer edges of the wings together. You will have to make a few tiny darts at the tips of the wings. Fit the rest of the chair as usual.

When you come to sew the cover, it is best to tack the wing seams after re-pinning them to the correct side in order to make sure that the darts stay in position.

Loose cover for a wing chair. Make sure the seams along the wings are snugly fitted before sewing. You may have to make a few darts at the tips to take up excess fabric. The rest of cover is fitted as usual.

Cover for a chair without arms

This too will usually have a plain hem with a tie-under finish, though a skirt would be perfectly feasible. The planning, cutting, fitting and sewing stages are as for a conventional arm chair. Be especially careful to get a good fit round the tuck-away areas.

Cover for a straight-sided chair

Again, all the same construction principles apply but you will need to make borders to go round the tops of the arms and back. The edges of the borders will be piped.

Sofa cover

Making a cover for a sofa or chesterfield is not much more difficult than for an armchair although the added bulk calls for even greater care in labelling the sections as you cut them out, and for methodical working in general. As with a chair, check first that the sofa is structurally sound, shampoo and mothproof it if necessary, and replace any broken casters.

There is not a great deal of extra necessary information if you follow the cardinal rules, such as measuring the sofa at its widest, longest and bulkiest points, cutting everything (except the piping casings) on the straight grain, and adding 2.5 cm to each seam and 5 cm to each hem edge.

When working out a cutting plan to estimate the quantity of fabric to buy, bear in mind that you will need to join widths of fabric to extend over the outside back, inside back, seat and front border. You can use for guidance any existing seams on the sofa; alternatively, if there are cushions, the seams should be lined up with the cushion edges. If you are using a fabric with a considerable pattern, you won't be able to match the pattern *and* follow these seam lines, so the solution is to pipe the seams. If there are no cushions, use a complete fabric width for the centre panels and join other smaller pieces to the sides to make up the required width, trying to achieve a continuity of pattern down the inside back, across the seat and down the front border. On a small two-seater sofa, it is best to have one central seam dividing the two sides.

If you want to give the sofa a straight-sided skirt with kick-pleats, you may want to have two extra pleats along the front and back lined up with the cushion edges or seams.

Remember to estimate enough fabric for the piping. If you feel you won't be able to make up enough from the surplus down the sides of the material, add up to 2 m to your total fabric requirement.

You must be prepared to adjust and readjust the cover at the pinning stage in order to get the best fit. It is worth spending a lot of time measuring and pinning so that when you do eventually sew the seams you will be confident that they are correct. You may find that tipping the sofa on its front helps, especially when fitting the outside back to the rest of the cover.

Sew with a double row of stitching those seams that will take a lot of wear, such as round the front of the arms, across the top of the back, along the front of the seat. Neaten all the seams by hand overcasting.

Instructions for making a skirt or plain hem with tie-unders and for the various types of opening are the same as for a chair loose cover.

Cushions

In most decorating schemes you can hardly have too many cushions. They are an excellent way of using up remnants, particularly expensive fabrics such as tapestry and silk. There are great savings to be had if you make your own cushions since bought ones are dear. Moreover, this is probably the area in soft furnishing where imagination and creativity can be best tapped. The possible shapes, styles and decorative effects are pretty well infinite. Cushions can be square, round, oval, heart-shaped, cylindrical; they can range in size from tiny scatter cushions to huge floor cushions; they can serve a specific purpose such as lining a window seat, forming a headrest at the back of a bed, or making a kitchen chair more comfortable; they can be utterly plain, or frilled, hand- or machine-embroidered, piped, overlaid with lace, include patchwork or quilting (see page 136) or appliqué work in their construction, have sequinned segments or buttoned, pleated or smocked areas – the range is virtually limitless.

The fabric you choose will obviously be important since smocking, for instance, would only be appropriate on a light fabric that wouldn't get much wear and tear, whereas the fabric for a cushion intended as a headrest would need to be hard-wearing. It is best to have washable fabrics, though cushions involving more complex construction techniques and expensive fabrics will need dry-cleaning.

Making the pad

Whichever style of cushion you are making, it is always best to make the inner pad as a separate element – otherwise you will never be able to clean the cover.

Any upholstery supplier should be able to provide you with a cushion interior or pad of an appropriate size and filling but you may want to make a pad to your particular requirements. The pad should be 1.25 cm *wider* in both directions than the cushion cover so that the finished object will look properly plump. This applies whether the filling is feathers or down, kapok or synthetic wadding. If the filling is in the form of plastic foam in block or chip form the pad should be the same size as the cushion cover.

Down　As with duvet fillings, down is the best but the most expensive choice. The pad casing should be made from downproof cambric and you should wax the stitching lines to prevent the quills poking through the holes. You will need about $\frac{1}{2}$ kg to stuff an average-sized cushion.

Feathers　These are the next best choice. You will need about 1 kg to fill an average-sized cushion, and the casing should be made from featherproof ticking. In this case, the outer cover should not be too thin or the black stripes on the ticking will show through. Waxing the seams would be a good idea here too.

Terylene and Dacron　These are cheaper substitutes but not so luxurious, and they don't plump up so well. They are washable, which may be an advantage, and the pad's cover can be made from cheap calico, old sheeting or curtain lining. You will need $\frac{1}{2}$ kg for an average-sized cushion.

Kapok tends to go lumpy and lose its shape, but would be a possibility on a purely decorative cushion rather than on a utilitarian one – you would need about $\frac{1}{2}$ kg for a small cushion.

Plastic foam　Whether in a block or chip form, this crumbles and rots if exposed to the sun, even protected by an outer cover, but is the cheapest alternative apart from the nearly as lumpy cut-up old tights. Blocks of foam are particularly useful for welted cushions and can be cut to the

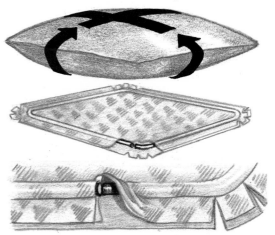

correct shape and size with a Stanley knife. For small bean bag you will need about 5 cubic feet of polystyrene beads for the filling.

To make the pad, cut out two pieces of ticking or calico (or whatever you are using) to the correct size, allowing 1.5 cm for turnings. See later in the section for how to get an accurate circle, and for guidance on cutting other shapes. Sew the pieces together in a French seam, wrong sides together first, leaving an opening about 15–20 cm long for inserting the stuffing. A French seam will lessen the likelihood of the pad bursting.

Turn the seam to the inside and fill the pad. This is best done in the garden or in the bathroom with the door shut, especially when feathers or polystyrene beads are involved. When the cushion is well filled, close the gap with oversewing, being particularly careful to secure the ends of the thread.

Cushion cover

Instructions follow for square, round, heart-shaped and cylindrical (bolster) covers, and for welted or boxed and squab cushions. Any decorative feature should be incorporated in the design before the cushion is made up.

Before you cut out the fabric, it is best to make a paper pattern in order to get the dimensions accurate; and if you use tracing or other semi-translucent paper (eg greaseproof) you will find it easier to centre any motifs in the fabric.

Square cushion

For a square cushion, measure the pad over the top from seam to seam. Don't measure the seams themselves. Cut two pieces of fabric with a 1.5 cm seam allowance all round. Remember that unless you are using a foam filling the finished cover should be very slightly smaller than the inner pad.

Square cushion. Measure round the fullest part of the cushion pad, not round the seams. If you are piping the cover, attach it to one section first – giving the square slightly rounded corners will help the piping to lie flat. Where the ends of the piping meet cut the cords (not the casings) so that they abut. Tuck the ends of the casings into the seam allowance.

Most cushions benefit in looks and strength by having piped edges (unless they are to have a frill or lace edging). Make up enough piping to go right round the cushion, plus about 3 cm. See page 80 for how to do this, and remember that if you plan to wash the cover, boil the cord first to prevent it shrinking later. The piping covering could be in a contrasting colour.

Piping on a square cushion will lie better if the corners are very slightly rounded. Use a saucer to draw round at each corner.

Make up the cushion by dealing with the piping first. Apply it round the seam line of one of the pieces of fabric, starting a few centimetres in from a corner. Never start it exactly at a corner or in the middle of a side: it will be either too weak or too conspicuous. Pin and machine-stitch it in place, joining the ends by cutting the cord (*not* the casing) of one end so that it abuts with the other end. Sew the ends together and tuck them into the seam allowance.

If you don't want to insert either a zip, a strip of Velcro or length of 'poppered' tape, all of which facilitate removal of the pad for cleaning, join the two halves of the cushion together round three sides and a short way along each end of the bottom edge. Neaten the raw edges and turn the cover right side out, insert the pad and slipstitch the opening together. When you come to clean the cover, unpick the handstitching to remove the pad.

Otherwise set in the means of opening the cover along the bottom edge of the cushion before dealing with the other seams. It should measure about 5 cm less than the edge. Start by joining only the two bottom edges together by stitching for 5 cm at each end, enclosing the piping neatly.

For a zip, turn under the raw, unpiped edge and tack it in place. Lay the closed zip under this edge, right side up. The centre of the teeth should be level with the tacked edge. Pin the zip in place and tack it. Bring the piped edge over the zip and tack along the edge of the piping. You could do the final sewing with the zipper (or piping) foot but you may find it easier in the long run to hand-sew the zip.

A strip of Velcro is a satisfactory alternative. Line up the outer edge of the Velcro with the piping stitching line. A further possibility is to use 'poppered' tape (the same as that used for duvet covers) or tape with hooks and eyes already sewn on. Attach the tape to the right side of the seam allowance of the opening making sure that the two sides of the tape correspond. Open the zip, Velcro or tape and sew twice round the other three sides of the cushion. This is particularly important on cushions which will take a great deal of wear. Clip the rounded corners and press and neaten the seams.

Round cushion

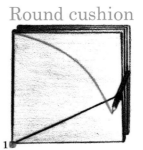

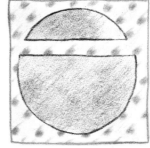

1 *Draw a circular template.*

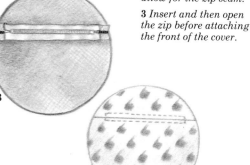

2 *Cut across the template a third of the way down. Arrange the sectors with a gap between them to allow for the zip seam.*

3 *Insert and then open the zip before attaching the front of the cover.*

Round cushions must be cut very accurately. For both the inner pad and the cover itself you will need to make a paper pattern (again, tracing paper will help for positioning motifs when you come to cut out the fabric). Decide on the diameter of the cushion and add 3 cm for seam allowances. Take a sheet of the paper you will be using for the pattern (it should be slightly larger than the finished cover) and fold it in four quarters. Tie a piece of string round a pencil and attach the string at the centre of the fold with a drawing-pin so that the length of the string is the radius of the cushion (half the measurement you took first). Draw round the arc as in fig 1. Cut round the pencil mark. When you open out the paper you should have a perfect circle.

As with square cushions, you have a choice of openings. The simplest is to leave a gap round a quarter of the circle for slipstitching closed when the cushion pad has been inserted. If you want to use a zip, Velcro or poppered tape, it is usual to apply it a third of the way down the back of the cover as it is not easy to insert a zip on a curve. The only disadvantage with this method is that the cushion will not be reversible – the zip side must always face towards the back.

Using the paper pattern, cut out what will be the front section of the cushion. Then draw a line across the pattern a third of the way down. Cut the circle into two and arrange the two sectors on the fabric so that they are separated by a 2.5 cm gap (fig 2). The gap represents the seam where the zip will be inserted. Cut round the sectors giving each the same 1.25 cm allowance along the gap. Right sides together, stitch across for a couple of centimetres at each end of the join. Insert a zip centrally over the seam, right side upwards, tacking and then machining it (fig 3).

If you are having piping, make up enough to fit round the circumference at the seam line and sew it to the other (front) section, first snipping into the seam allowance so that it will lie flat.

Open the zip and pin the front and back of the cover right sides together. Stitch round the seam line right up next to the piping. Clip the curves and turn and press the cover. The pad should slot comfortably through the opening.

Heart-shaped cushion

For a heart-shaped scatter cushion the same principle applies for inserting a zip – it should be at the widest point across the back, and in this case run the full width of the cushion. In order to make the template you will have to experiment but when you have arrived at the approximate shape and size, fold in half a piece of paper that is slightly larger than you want the finished cushion to be, and draw a half-heart so that when the paper is opened out the two sides will be symmetrical (fig 4). In other respects the construction is the same as for a round cushion.

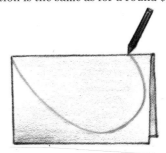

4 *Draw a heart-shaped template by folding a piece of paper in half and drawing half the heart.*

The zip should be inserted at the widest part of the back.

Bolster

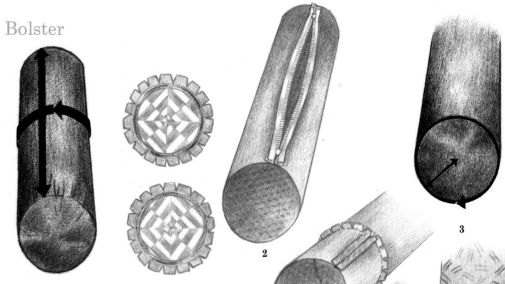

1 *Measure the length and girth of the bolster pad – the end circles will have the same diameter as the girth. Apply any piping to the end pieces first.*

2 *Insert the zip by hand. Open it before sewing on the end pieces.*

3 *For gathered ends, cut two strips of fabric the width of the radius and the length of the girth. Join the short sides of the strip; sew it to the bolster tube; then gather round the raw edge and draw up the gathers tightly. Sew on a button to cover the centre point.*

These long, thin cushions were traditionally used as head supports on sofas and couches. They are generally firmer than ordinary cushions so pack the filling tightly.

You will need to cut three main pieces of fabric whether you are making the inner pad or the cover. The largest piece will be the length of the finished bolster (plus 2.5 cm for seams) by the circumference required. The end circles will have the same diameter (fig 1). Make a paper pattern for the ends in the manner described for round cushions. If you are using piping apply it to the ends before they are joined to the main section. Clip round the curves before sewing.

The zip or other means of fastening should be inserted first. The opening must be quite long – certainly more than half the bolster's circumference. Position the zip centrally and hand-sew it in place. If you try to machine-sew it you may have trouble preventing several layers of fabric getting in the way of the machine's needle.

Open the fastening and sew the circular ends to the bolster, clipping into the seam allowances all round (fig 2). Open the cover right side out and insert the pad.

If you would prefer to have a bolster with gathered ends, instead of cutting circular end pieces cut a strip of fabric for each end as long as the circumference of the bolster and as wide as the radius, both plus 2.5 cm for turnings. Join the short sides of the strip and tack one of the long edges to the end of the tube, adding in any piping. Sew round the seam twice for strength. Run a row of gathering stitch (in the same colour as the fabric) along the other long end and draw it up tightly (fig 3). Fasten the thread securely. Snip round the curves as usual before turning the cover right side out and sewing a tassel or button over the centre to hide the raw edges of the gathers.

Welted or box cushions

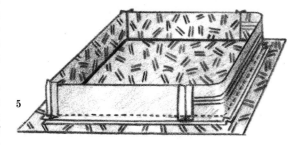

1 *Measure the dimensions of the cushion to be covered.*

2 *Join the front and side welts.*

3 *The zip is fitted horizontally halfway down the back welt, which is formed by two half-welts.*

4 *The zip welt carries round to the sides to allow the cushion pad to be removed easily. The front seams occur at the corners.*

5 *Join any piping to the flat panels before pinning and sewing the welt sections to them.*

Welted cushions can be square, rectangular round or shaped to fit the contours of an arm-chair. If you are making one from scratch the best filling to use is plastic foam in block form which can be shaped with a sharp blade.

You are more likely to want to cover the existing cushions on a chair or sofa – in this case vacuum and even shampoo the old cushions when you are preparing the rest of the chair.

Measure the width, length and depth of the cushion to be covered. Cut a top and a bottom piece, and give them slightly rounded corners so that the piping will lie easily. You may want to ensure that any pattern matches up with the chair's inside back panel and the front border.

You will also need to cut fabric for the welt. On a square or rectangular cushion the zip goes at the centre back, and carries round by about 5 cm to each side. So for the zip welt cut two strips of fabric, each the length of the back plus 5 cm, plus 2.5 cm for turnings; their width should be half the depth of the cushion plus 2.5 cm for turnings.

The three remaining welt sections are cut so that any pattern runs vertically. The front one will be the width of the cushion plus turnings. The other two will run from the front corners to the start of the zip welt (fig 5).

The construction order is: zip inserted into its two half-welts; all the welts joined together in the correct order; piping sewn to both top and bottom sections; welt section stitched to bottom of cover; top cover added to the rest to complete the project. Clip into the curves and snip off the corners as you go, and press the seams.

The only difference when making a round welted cushion is that the zip goes round half the diameter. Its part of the welt is formed in two sections as in fig 3.

For any other shape, for instance a back cushion with indents for the chair arms, it is best to insert the zip across the widest part of the back, adapting the principle outlined for round cushions on page 94.

Squab cushion

Squab cushions fit simple wooden chairs and are tied on with ribbons. The padding can be thin or plump as you prefer. For a single cushion you will need 2.4 m of ribbon to match or contrast with your fabric.

Lay a sheet of tracing or greaseproof paper over the seat of the chair and draw round its shape. At the same time mark where the ribbons are to go so that they can tie in pairs round each leg. Cut out a top and bottom piece for the cover, transfer the ribbon positions, and lay the pieces right sides together. Cut the ribbon into lengths of 30 cm and pin one at each mark, one end level with the edges of the fabric (fig 1). Sew round the seam, leaving a gap at the back edge through which the cushion pad can be inserted. Turn the cover right sides out, press it, insert the pad and slipstitch the gap closed.

If you want the cushion to be easily removable for laundering, insert a zip across the middle of the bottom half, adapting the principle given for a round cushion on page 94.

1 *Attach the ribbons for a squab cushion cover by pinning a length to each side of the corners, level with the edge of the fabric.*

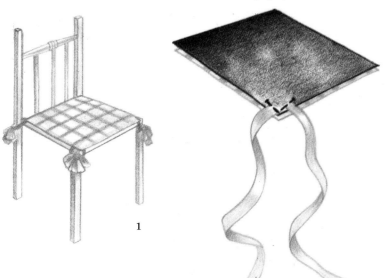

1

Decorative techniques for cushions

Patchwork and quilting (see page 136) lend themselves particularly well to cushion design, a major advantage being that even a small amount of work can be shown off to great effect.

Another decorative finish would be to make the front of a round cushion in the same way as for the buttoned end of the bolster cover on page 96, so that the gathered centre radiates outwards.

Or you could consider giving a cushion a frilled edging like that described for a pillowcase on page 45, or you could simply insert ruched lace edging between the top and bottom cover pieces before sewing them together.

There is one particularly useful technique applicable to cushion-making. This is the insertion of a panel so that it is framed by the rest of the cover. The panel can consist of smocking, patchwork, bead or appliqué work, embroidery – whatever you like. You could make it in a 'reverse' fabric of the rest of the cover, such as green flowers on a white background set into white flowers on a green background. Another punchy design would be to have a large chintz bird or flower set into a plain background, perhaps with an additional border framing it. If you have a lace panel back the lace with another fabric before you set it in the cushion.

Decide on the size of the panel and allow 1.5 cm all round for seam allowances. Also decide on the finished size of the cushion and cut two pieces for the cover to those measurements plus 1.5 cm all round. If either or both the panel and the cover are to be round see page 94 for how to cut out accurate circles.

Lay the panel either straight or diagonally on top of what will be the top section of the cover and draw round it with dressmaker's chalk. Draw another box or shape of the panel 3 cm inside those chalked lines (fig 2). Cut out the material from within this second chalk line. Draw in a third line halfway between the first two. Cut diagonally into the corners as far as this third line and press the seam allowance under by 1.5 cm.

Pin the panel under the 'frame' and slipstitch it in place (fig 3). You may have to strengthen the corners with extra stitching where you cut into the seam allowance. If the panel is not hand-worked, you could attach it by machine top-stitching or zigzagging.

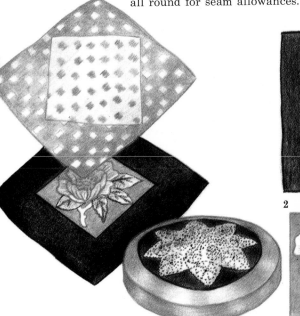

2

3

2 Lay the panel on the fabric and draw round its edge. Draw another line 3 cm inside the first box. Cut out along this second line. A third line is drawn halfway between the two – cut diagonally into the corners at this third line.

3 Fold under the allowance you have made. Fit the panel under the frame and slipstitch it in place.

Pouffe

You may want only to make a new cover for an existing pouffe – see below. To make a new pouffe itself, you will need a hard-wearing fabric such as repp, heavy chintz or even suede – a metre of 120 cm fabric will probably be enough; the same amount of calico for lining material; strong canvas for the base; a sheet of stiff cardboard; flock, wood shavings or other firm filling; and piping cord. You may find a curved upholstery needle a help, particularly on suede. Plan any decorative features such as quilting (page 136) or appliqué work before you cut and sew the pieces.

For a round pouffe cut the top to your required size plus 1.25 cm all round for seam allowances. See page 94 for how to make a circular template. The sides are made in two panels. Each panel should be the depth of the finished pouffe plus 10 cm, and the length of half the circumference of the top plus 2.5 cm for seam allowances. There should be ample material left over from the metre to cut bias strips for piping.

a *fabric*

b *calico lining*

c *canvas*

d *cardboard*

e *wood shavings*

f *piping cord*

g *curved upholstery needle*

1 *The pieces to cut for a pouffe: 2 main panels, 2 lining panels, 1 main top, 2 lining tops, 1 cardboard top, 1 canvas base*

Cut two sides and *two* tops from the calico, and one top from the cardboard (fig 1). The canvas circle base should be slightly smaller than these – dock about 2 cm from the diameter.

Make up enough piping to go round the top edge – see page 80. Pin the piping to the circle of main fabric, tack it if you want, and stitch round, clipping into the seam allowances to allow the layers to lie properly. Join the side seams of the panels, then join the panels to the top, clipping into their allowances likewise.

Make up the lining in the same stages (skipping the piping). Turn both the cover and the lining right sides out and fit the lining inside the cover. It will help to anchor the two pieces with invisible stitching where the side seams meet the circles (fig 2).

Fill the pouffe, making sure that there is sufficient round the top seam. Pack in the filling very firmly – if there is not enough the pouffe will soon sag. When the filling is 7 cm from the open edges, insert the cardboard and pull the lining panels over it by drawing across double threads (fig 3). Turn under 1.25 cm round the remaining calico circle by pressing or tacking – snip into

the seam allowance. Stitch it to the drawn-up lining panels – you may find the curved needle a help here (fig 4).

Draw up the outer panels similarly (fig 5). Turn under the seam allowance of the canvas base, again snipping into it, and stitch it centrally with double thread (fig 6). The pouffe is now finished, although you could clinch in its waist with a tasselled cord.

A square or oblong pouffe can be made following the same principles. Gently round the corners by drawing round a saucer so that the piping will lie properly. Insert piping down the four corner seams as well if you want.

For a separate loose cover, cut fabric to match the top and side panels, taking seam turnings into account, and allowing about 5 cm for a double 1.5 cm hem and 2 cm to go under the pouffe. Make up the cover as if you were making the pouffe itself; then turn up the double hem. Sew six tapes at equal intervals round the bottom of the hem so that they can tie centrally under the pouffe (fig 6). Alternatively, you can insert a length of elastic into the double hem and gather it up so that the cover fits snugly.

5

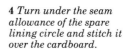

6

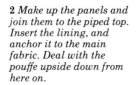

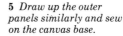

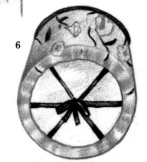

4

2 *Make up the panels and join them to the piped top. Insert the lining, and anchor it to the main fabric. Deal with the pouffe upside down from here on.*

3 *Fill the pouffe tightly. Insert the cardboard. Draw up the lining with threads running across.*

4 *Turn under the seam allowance of the spare lining circle and stitch it over the cardboard.*

5 *Draw up the outer panels similarly and sew on the canvas base.*

6 *A loose cover can be tied on with tapes underneath.*

101

Stool

Stools and boxes of any shape can be given loose covers to protect them and to link them in with the rest of the decorating scheme. A round stool for a bedroom may look best with a gathered skirt extending from the base of the seat, whereas a lower stool with a larger seat area or a footstool may call for more tailored box pleats or inverted corner pleats.

Choose fabric which is hard-wearing enough to be sat on constantly and yet which drapes well. As with larger loose covers, sensible choices would be linen union, damask, heavy cotton or a not-too-thick repp. You may in any case have enough left over after re-covering your chair or sofa. You will probably want to pipe the main edges (see page 80).

Before you cover the stool, check to see that its structure is sound. If the seat has sunk a bit you could incorporate a layer of synthetic wadding in the loose cover to build it up.

Cut out pieces of fabric to correspond to the areas to be covered: seat, side borders, skirt, and bias strips for piping. Fabric for the sides and skirt should be cut so that the pattern runs vertically, and the seat should have any major motif positioned centrally.

Fit and make up the cover starting with the seat, padding and lining it if necessary. Then sew the piping to it before you tackle the sides. Sew on the skirt last – see pages 87 and 88 for how to make the different types of skirt. Neaten the seams with hand overcasting. You don't need to include a zip in the cover as it should slip off quite easily for cleaning.

Canvas chairs

1

Deckchair

For re-covering an old deckchair you will need canvas to replace the old material, some 10 mm tacks, a hammer and a screwdriver. With the aid of the screwdriver, gouge out the old tacks that are keeping the canvas in place. Buy new canvas to the same length, remembering to take the turnings into account.

At each end fold under 2.5 cm to the wrong side and press it in place. Lay the fabric right side down on the floor and sort the deckchair out on top so that it too is facing downwards.

Bring the top end of the canvas round the top bar and hammer in a tack at the middle point (fig 1). Be sure that it is straight and taut before hammering in further tacks at each end of the bar, and then more to fill in the gaps. You should aim to fix a tack every 5 or 6 cm.

Repeat the exercise for the bottom bar. The deckchair's construction is such that this bar is slightly narrower so you will have to fold the canvas under at each side by about 2 cm (fig 2).

Director's chair

To remove the old canvas cut away from the frame using a Stanley knife. Then cut round the canvas as near as possible to the nails, but don't try to gouge out the nails themselves or you may split the wood. Instead, hammer them flush with or into the surface of the wood.

Measure for the seat material before you ease the back off the uprights – otherwise the chair will collapse making measuring difficult. Measure across from the outside of one side bar to the equivalent place on the other bar, and add

on about 5 cm to the length. Use the old canvas as a pattern to gauge the width, adding 4 cm for hems front and back. Likewise, use the back of the chair as a gauge for the material to buy, adding on 5 cm for turning under at the sides. Add on 3 cm to the depth.

When you cut out the fabric, contrive that the top of the back will have a selvedge. If you are using striped canvas be particularly careful that you cut both pieces quite straight.

Deal with the back first. Turn under and press the selvedge by 1 cm. On the opposite sides turn under a double 1 cm hem. Machine-stitch along both these hems. Turn under and press 1 cm at both short ends. Then using the chair uprights as guides pin the fold to the back of the fabric to form casings (fig 3). Machine the casings.

Give the seat double 1 cm hems turned under along the front and back edges. Press under 2.5 cm at each side, then collapse the chair and hammer in tacks through the hem every 5 or 6 cm on the underside of the bar, being careful to avoid the old tacks. Finish the other side in the same way.

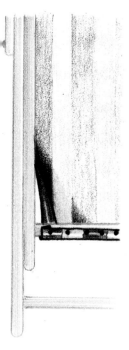

1 *Bring the folded-under end of the canvas round the top bar. Hammer in a tack at the mid-point before adding further tacks the length of the bar.*

2 *The bottom bar is narrower so fold under the canvas a little at each side.*

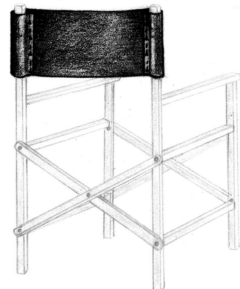

3 *Deal with the back of the director's chair before the seat. Use the uprights as guides for making casings of the correct width.*

Cover for an ottoman

1

Many a household has an ottoman, an old chest or a lidded box useful for storing linen and for sitting on. Unless it is a beautiful antique it may well benefit from being covered in fabric.

Check first that the box's structure is sound and that the hinges are in working order. You will need enough fabric to cover the top and the four sides – allow extra for centring any motifs. The fabric will hang next to the wood so if you want to achieve a softer look you could use quilted material. Buy enough lining fabric to fit the bottom and sides of the box, and for the underside of the lid if you don't want to use rather smarter black upholstery lining there. You will also need enough foam (1.5 cm thick) and strong cardboard to line the bottom and sides of the box; upholstery tacks; a hammer, glue, and braid to go round the inner top edge of the box and round the lid. If you are giving a flat box a buttoned top you will need in addition chipboard the same dimensions as the lid, a drill, broad-headed tacks, a long upholstery needle and strong thread, and, for deep buttoning, a couple of kitchen spoons.

First cut the fabric into four outer panels for the front, back and two sides of the box, with 2.5 cm seam allowances where the panels will meet at the corners, and a 2.5 cm allowance along the bottom edges. At the top, allow enough extra fabric to turn under the top edges and fit inside, plus a 2.5 cm hem allowance.

For the inside of the box use a standard curtain lining fabric in a colour complementary to the outer fabric. The look of the lining will be improved if it is lightly padded with foam covered board. For this cut a rectangle of strong cardboard or thin hardboard to fit the bottom of the box. Glue to it a rectangle of 1.5 cm thick foam of the same size. Cut a piece of lining fabric

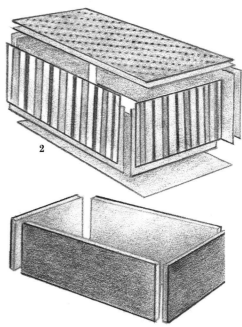

2

1 *Measure the dimensions of the box or ottoman.*

2 *Cut panels of outer fabric, lining, foam and cardboard. Don't forget to cut panels of linings, foam and cardboard for the inside bottom of the box.*

to the same size, adding 2.5 cm allowances all round, and stretch it over the foam-covered board. Glue the turnings to the board, mitring the corners.

Cut four further pieces of board, foam and lining fabric to fit the inner sides of the box, and cover them similarly. You can either fit them individually or sew them all together. To fit them individually, push a tack through the covered panel near each corner. Hammer it home using a block to prevent the hammer damaging the fabric (fig 3). To fit the lining panels together, hand-sew the edges to form a box-like structure and lower it into the ottoman (fig 4).

Sew the outer panels into one continuous band of fabric, right sides together. Slide it on to the box and adjust it to fit at the corners. Mitre and slipstitch the fabric over the top edges of the box sides; turn the raw edges under where the outside fabric meets the lining, and slipstitch the two together all round. A simple length of braid sewn round the inside top edge will give a neat finish and conceal the join (fig 5). Turn the bottom edge under, and hammer in tacks all round the base of the ottoman.

The cover for the lid may have a similar panel of padded lining underneath, with a top outer cover slipstitched to it. If the box or ottoman lid is fairly deep, trim and sew the corners of the top cover to fit. Press under the allowances of the lining and slipstitch it down over the raw edges of the top cover. The fabric will have to be trimmed and turned under round the hinges. A length of braid slipstitched round the edge of the lid gives a good finish.

For any flat-topped ottoman, a panel of 5 cm foam fixed in place with a few spots of glue turns it into a convenient seat. If you are making up a box of your own, you can improve its appearance with a simple pattern of buttoning. The simplest top is a flat rectangle of chipboard.

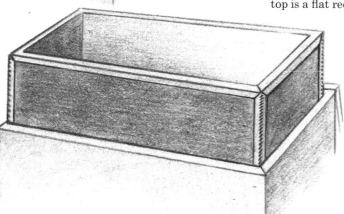

3

4

5

3 *If you fit the inner panels individually, hammer in a tack at each corner using a block to protect the fabric.*

4 *Or sew all the individually constructed lining panels together before lowering them into the ottoman.*

5 *A simple way of finishing the inside top edge is to sew on a length of braid.*

Loose covers and cushions

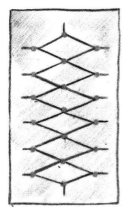

1 *Experiment with patterns of buttoning for a padded lid, and sketch in the pleats between them.*

Start by drawing a pattern of button points, and sketch in the pleats between them. An example is given in fig 1. An upholstery materials supplier will provide you with buttons and he may also cover them for you if you take along a length of the fabric; or you can buy buttons for covering yourself from any large haberdashery department.

At the points where the buttons will fit, drill holes through the chipboard. Next to each hole hammer halfway home on the underside a short broad-headed upholstery tack. Glue the foam in place and lay the covering fabric loosely over it. Hammer in a couple of tacks or drawing-pins to hold the fabric while you work.

Starting at the centre buttonhole, sew up from the back of the hole through the board, the foam and the top cover. Use a good strong upholstery thread, because the buttons will be subjected to considerable strain. Thread the loop of the button on to the thread, and take the needle back down through the fabric and the foam, using a slightly different path. Return through the hole in the board, pull the thread taut, and tie the ends firmly round the tack next to the hole (fig 2).

Move on to the next hole and sew up through it and the foam. Draw the fabric firmly into place, press it down over the needle, draw the needle through, thread on the button, and return the thread through the fabric and foam. Pull the thread taut, and secure it round the tack. When you are confident that you have got the set of the fabric right and will not have to rework the button, hammer home both tacks.

If you are using very thick foam, the fabric will need pleating between the button points, and the effect will be deep buttoning. To shape the pleats you need a couple of spoons. Using the handles tuck one under the pleat between the two buttons and hold the other over the pleat. Slide them gently along the fabric in the same direction to form a neat and tidy pleat (fig 3).

Go on to a third buttonhole. Sew and secure the button, and tidy up the pleat as you go. As the pattern spreads, you will have more than one pleat at some buttons. Remember to tidy the pleats before you proceed too far or the pleat will become inaccessible.

When you have completed the pattern, turn the fabric over the edges of the board, and mitre the corners. Apply your lining, turning under and hand-sewing the edges. Ordinary lining fabric is acceptable for the job, but you will achieve a much smarter finish with stiff black upholstery lining. Fold it to the right dimensions to lie neatly within the edges of the board, and secure it with small, broad-headed upholstery tacks at intervals of about 2.5 cm.

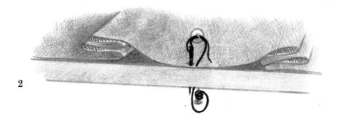

2

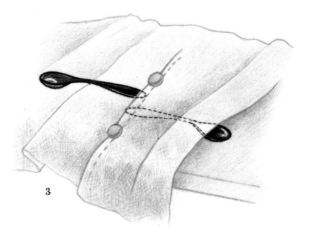

3

2 *Sew up through the central hole drilled in the board, bring the needle up through the layers, through the button and down again. Secure the thread to the tack next to the hole.*

3 *Smooth out the pleats with a pair of spoon handles. Complete each pleat as you go along while it is still accessible.*

Lampshades

Making lampshades is one of the most rewarding activities in soft furnishing, especially from the creative and financial points of view. If you have the patience, you can produce exquisite shades to almost any design you like. The work is delicate and small in scale but vitally important to any decorating scheme. If you get the lighting right, a room will look at its best; if the lighting is wrong, even the most expensive and elegant furnishings can look dead and uninviting. In terms of money, the savings in this area are perhaps greater than in any other branch of soft furnishing: the lampshade takes so little material that you can make it at little cost, using left-over pieces of fabric.

The range of lampshade shapes is extensive, and choice of fabric to cover them almost infinite. It is best to acquire some experience by making a simple shade first so that you learn what kinds of effect can be achieved. Experiment with scraps of material held in front of a naked bulb, bearing in mind the purpose of the lamp. If it is a reading lamp, avoid dark colours unless the shape of the frame allows a wide diffusion of light at the bottom. Whites and reds shed a rather harsh light (though white can be warmed up with a coloured lining), and blues a cool one. Popular colours are various shades of pink, apricot, yellow and cream, all of which create a warm effect.

Tapered drum
lampshade 111

Pleated lampshades 117

Square lampshade
116

Plain designs are usually the most effective as well as the most efficient. In any case, the light will show up any construction defects which are more likely to occur with a complicated design.

The fabric should be washable and strong enough to be stretched on to the frame, but not too thick. For these reasons crêpe-backed satin, silk shantung and wild silk are extravagant but very good choices for a tailored lampshade. Taffeta and lining fabrics wear too easily and show pin marks. Gathered tiffany lampshades look good in dress cottons, lawn and gingham or, for a still more delicate effect, in lined broderie anglaise and lace. If you are making a pleated shade you will need silk chiffon or another soft fabric that drapes well.

For firm lampshades (see page 121) milliner's buckram on its own makes an effective homespun-looking shade, or can be used to stiffen paper, lace or other soft fabric.

Whichever fabric you choose, make sure that it is not easily flammable – it will be close to a hot light bulb. Buy a lining to tone with the fabric – flame-proof linings are obtainable and although a crêpe lining is the best, cotton lawn and fine lawn are also suitable. Make it clear to the sales assistant that the fabric is for a lampshade lining.

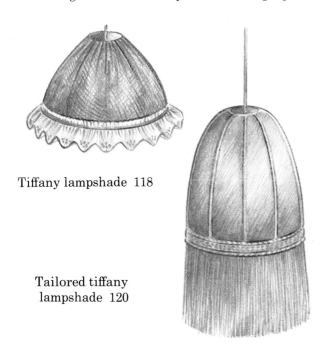

Tiffany lampshade 118

Tailored tiffany
lampshade 120

Handkerchief
lampshade 120

Firm lampshades 121

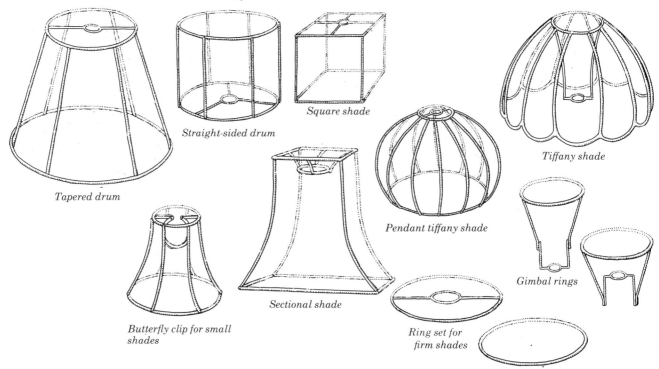

Tapered drum

Straight-sided drum

Square shade

Tiffany shade

Pendant tiffany shade

Gimbal rings

Butterfly clip for small shades

Sectional shade

Ring set for firm shades

Tools and materials for fabric lampshades

The basis of any lampshade is the frame, obtainable in the furnishing department of most stores and at many small shops that specialise in household furnishings. The frame is a strong structure in copper or steel wire with, typically, a ring at the top and bottom, and several upright struts, all welded together. In the middle is a lampholder, often an adjustable gimbal so that the shade will tilt to throw light at a particular angle.

Choose the frame in conjunction with the base of the lamp before you make the shade – otherwise the proportions may turn out unbalanced. Check that it has the correct fitting for a standard or floor lamp, a table lamp, or a clip-on or hanging (pendant) lamp. Soft fabric shades will need a strutted frame as well as rings top and bottom, while firm shades need only a ring set with the appropriate fitting (a strutted frame can be used but is not essential). Large frames can be difficult for a beginner to handle, so pick a small frame of a relatively straightforward shape. Avoid the small 'candle-shade' frames – they are the most tricky of all to handle.

You may want to resurrect an old frame – see below (under Binding the frame) for the way to prepare it.

You will also need binding tape. Standard white tape about 1–1.5 cm wide is fine if you can't buy unbleached loose-woven lampshade tape. Buy $2\frac{1}{2}$ times the total length of the circumference of the rings and the length of all the struts, measured generously. You will not need to bind the bulb fitting. Buy also a cold-water dye to make the bound frame the same colour as the main fabric. You may be tempted to use bias binding in a colour already matching your fabric or lining – if you do, iron out one of the creased edges before using it.

Small fine-gauge pins are essential, no longer than 2.5 cm (smaller than some dressmaking pins). Other necessary pieces of equipment are sharps needles (grades 3–9) for fabric lampshades, and betweens needles (5–6) for firm shades; a fabric tape measure; dressmaking scissors (and nail scissors are also useful); adhesive such as Uhu or Copydex for fixing certain trimmings; a metal file or fine sandpaper; and quick-drying enamel paint or plastic varnish if you are using an old frame. You will also need lengths of string and 7.5 mm elastic for a gathered tiffany shade.

Finally, you will probably want to trim the top and bottom edges of the shade with a braid or fringe. There is a huge variety to choose from but again, the simpler ones tend to be the most effective, perhaps a plain braid about 5–10 mm wide in a colour toning with the main fabric.

Binding the frame

There are two schools of thought on how to prepare a frame. Some lampshade-makers prefer to bind tape round the entire metal part to help prevent the hard profile showing through the fabric. Others find this unnecessary. Many frames are already coated in white plastic or enamel when you buy them, and the full binding then becomes superfluous. Even so, you will have to bind the top and bottom rings and the vertical struts at two opposite sides to give you a base to pin the fabric to.

The best plan is to bind your first frame all round. You can then decide whether you would prefer to use partially bound frames on later projects.

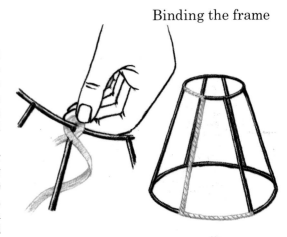

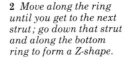

1 *Start binding at the top of the frame where a strut meets the ring. Hold the tape against the inside of the frame, pull the other end out over the top and down through the centre to secure the first end.*

2 *Move along the ring until you get to the next strut; go down that strut and along the bottom ring to form a Z-shape.*

3 *To turn at a corner.*

First, take a file or sandpaper to the frame and file down any sharp corners – not right through to the joint, just enough to round off the hard edge. On an old frame with all the previous trimmings removed, sandpaper off any rust and paint the frame with plastic varnish or enamel paint. This is especially important if you are going eventually to wash the shade. On a new shade with plastic coating, shave off with a razor blade or sharp knife any lumps of excess plastic, particularly round the joints. Make sure that any movable parts on a gimbal fitting are free-moving, and correct any misalignments in the frame, likely on an old frame, by gently bending the metal.

Measure along the top of the frame between two struts, down one of them and along the bottom of the frame between the two uprights.

Multiply this length by 2½, and cut off that much tape from your roll. This will be as much as you will be able to handle at one time. Start at the inside top of the frame where a strut meets the top ring, with the tape held against the inside of the frame. Pull the tape out over the frame and down through the centre, to secure the end (fig 1 on the previous page). Make a few turns along the ring, sloping each one away from the starting point at an acute angle and keeping the tape taut. You will see now why you do not want to handle too much tape at any one time – the long length can become inconvenient. Some people wind the tape round a small card but you will probably find it easier to throw the loose end over and pull it through, rather than to bother unravelling the tape from the card.

The other problem which you will soon encounter is that the tape tends to gape at the overlaps. You must make the elasticity of the tape work to eliminate this gaping as much as you can, stretching and pulling the tape to make it lie flat against the previous turn. Make the binding as neat and flat as possible with the same overlap all along and avoiding double overlaps which will produce too much bulk.

You will arrive at the first upright strut: the binding must go down that strut, then along the bottom ring, to form a Z-shape (fig 2 on previous page). For turning the corner, simply bind one turn beyond the strut, then reverse the binding, take the tape behind the upright, and start winding down the upright itself so that you effect a figure of eight (fig 3 on previous page).

Bind down the upright, turn the corner, and go along to the next corner. If your original measuring was accurate and your binding has been neat, you should end up with just the right amount to reach that corner. If you have too much, go back and check that you have no serious gaps, and rework the length. If it falls short, you will almost certainly have the tape with too little stretch along the frame, resulting in too much bulk. You will probably find small gaps at the corners, where the frame shows through. This doesn't matter as the gaps will be covered later by other lengths of tape.

When you come to the end of the first length and are satisfied with the neatness of the binding, pin the tape to itself and cut a new length. Start it at the top of the frame to meet the first length of binding, and follow the same Z-shape. At the bottom of the second upright, you will encounter the end of the first length of tape. Take out the pin, and bind the second tape round the first as you did at the previous corner. Each length of tape will secure the length before it. Eventually you will come to the bottom of your first upright strut. Pin that last length in place, then sew it for a firm fixing, making the stitches on the outside of the frame – these will be hidden by the outer fabric. The cover of the shade will itself fix the binding in place all round. The binding should be quite taut and firm so that the cover will not slip at all.

Now is the time to dye the bound frame to the required colour of the main fabric or lining, using a cold-water dye.

The cover

Let us assume that you have a frame which is wider at the bottom than at the top and which has six panels – an empire frame. Many shades are made to this pattern. Take the measurement of three panels, round the bottom of the frame. Measure the height of the frame. Add a generous 10 cm to both measurements. This should be enough to cater for any curve in the upright struts. If the curve is pronounced and the shade a large one, add a little more to make sure you do not skimp when buying the material. You can now cut a rectangle to cover three panels (half) of the frame.

The selvedge or straight grain of the material should run from top to bottom, unless the shape

Start fitting the fabric over the three panels of the frame. Insert a pin through the fabric and the binding at the four corners. The fabric should be quite taut. Gradually pin round to fill in the gaps – the pins should face in the directions shown.

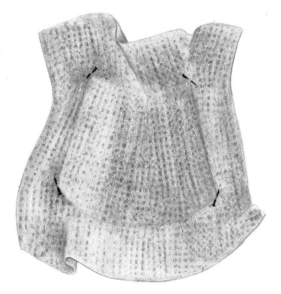

of the frame is waisted. If that is the case, give yourself greater flexibility by cutting the material on the bias – that is, the grain of the fabric should run diagonally to the sides of the rectangle; alternatively, the rectangle should be laid out diagonally to the length of the piece of fabric.

Now you can start to fit the covering fabric to the frame. Spread the fabric over the frame to cover the three panels as accurately as you can. The fabric must overhang the frame on all sides. Insert a pin through the fabric and the binding at the four corners. Draw the fabric fairly taut, and pin it to the binding with three more pins each at top and bottom. Pins along the top and bottom rings should face into the middle, and those down the sides should face outwards (see fig). This is to lessen damage to both you and the shade. If you do prick your finger and get blood on to the fabric, moisten some tacking cotton and dab it at once on to the bloodstain.

Pin the fabric in place to the two uprights.

Unpin the top, ease and draw up the fabric, and pin it again. That will probably throw the fabric out of shape between the top and bottom rings so unpin it at one or the other, ease out any ruckles, and re-pin it. Go on unpinning, easing and drawing the fabric, and re-pinning until you eliminate all the ruckles and bulges. Eventually you should achieve a straight, crease-free covering over that half of the frame, without stretching the fabric unreasonably. The pins will be at intervals of about 5 mm. If you have done the job badly you will see that the fabric is pulled out of shape and you may even find that you have drawn the fabric so tight you have pulled the frame out of shape. If so, take off the fabric, straighten the frame, and start again.

When you are satisfied, trim off the surplus fabric to 2.5 cm from the frame all round. Mark the position of the frame. Dressmaker's chalk is the best marking tool for fabric, but you could also use a pencil lightly. Rub it over the fabric along the line of the frame all round, then take

Lampshades

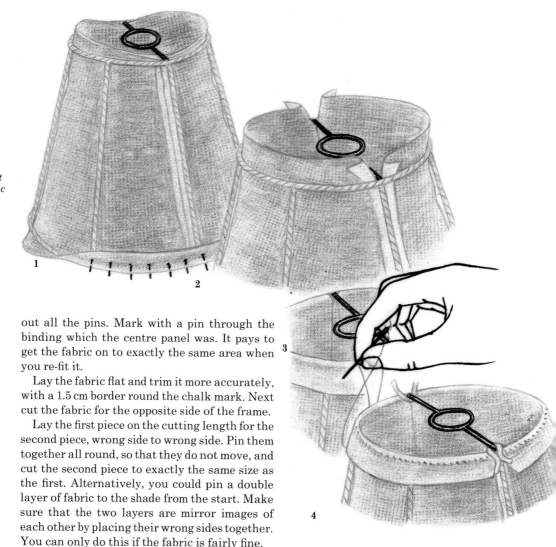

1 *Open out the lining inside the frame. The seams should face outwards and coincide with the struts. Line up the horizontal chalk marks with the top and the bottom. Turn the excess over the bottom ring and hold it in place with a few pins through the binding.*

2 *Ease the lining through to the top ring. Unpick the seams a short distance so that the fabric can be drawn up round the lamp fittings. Fold the excess over to the outside.*

out all the pins. Mark with a pin through the binding which the centre panel was. It pays to get the fabric on to exactly the same area when you re-fit it.

Lay the fabric flat and trim it more accurately, with a 1.5 cm border round the chalk mark. Next cut the fabric for the opposite side of the frame.

Lay the first piece on the cutting length for the second piece, wrong side to wrong side. Pin them together all round, so that they do not move, and cut the second piece to exactly the same size as the first. Alternatively, you could pin a double layer of fabric to the shade from the start. Make sure that the two layers are mirror images of each other by placing their wrong sides together. You can only do this if the fabric is fairly fine.

The lining

A balloon lining is a standard lining fixed top and bottom to the frame. Fold the lining fabric in half, wrong sides together and so that the

3 *Oversew the lining to the binding all round with very small stitches on the outside of the rings.*

4 *Cut two strips of lining fabric to tie round and conceal the gaps where the lamp fittings occur. Trim the lining fabric close to the sewing line.*

straight grain of the fabric will run from top to bottom of the shade. Lay the pinned outer fabric on top of it. Cut the doubled lining to exactly the same size.

Return to the outer panels and re-pin them along the marked line; then machine-sew them together, right side to right side, along the chalked or pencilled guideline. Stretch the fabric slightly as you go – this will avoid the stitches breaking later when the cover is pulled over the frame. Sew the lining into a similar tube, but a fraction smaller than the outer fabric, and mark with chalk or pencil the top and bottom of the frame.

Trim off the excess on the two parts of the outer cover and lining to 5 mm from the seams only, not at the top and bottom. Then press the cover flat but do not open the seams. The cover is now ready for fitting.

Start with the lining. Open it out inside the frame, wrong side towards the frame, and make sure that the seams coincide with those struts where the seams in the outer fabric will eventually fall. Line up the horizontal chalk or pencil marks with the top and bottom of the frame (fig 1).

Turn the excess over the bottom ring and put in a few pins on the outside edge to hold it in place to the binding. Invert the frame, and ease the lining through tidily to the smaller top ring. Draw it tight but not too taut. At the sides, where the lampholder is welded on, unpick the seam just enough to allow you to bring the fabric up round the junction of the frame and gimbal or lampholder. Turn under the raw edges round the cut, and fold the excess fabric over to the outside of the ring (fig 2). Do not pull it too hard, or you will force the bottom fabric out of place. Put a few pins into the binding. Then start shaping the lining by taking out a few pins, easing it gradually more tautly top and bottom, and re-pin. Go all round, aiming to get a good set to the fabric. Be prepared to work at it, pulling out any

unevenness and eliminating any ruckles.

When you are satisfied with the way the lining sits, oversew it to the binding all round with very small stitches. Your sewing lines should be on the outside edges of the rings (fig 3). Later those areas will be covered so the stitches will not be visible.

Cut two new rectangles of the lining fabric, each 10 cm by 4 cm. Fold each one into three along its length and thread them under the struts of the lampholder, one on each side. Turn them over to the outside of the frame, pin them in place and sew them, again on the outside edge of the top ring. They conceal the gap which you made to fit the lining fabric up into the angle of the gimbal or lampholder. Trim the lining fabric close to the sewing line (fig 4).

Fitting the cover

Now slide on the outer cover. Adjust it so that the panels lie where you originally fitted them. The seams of the outer cover and lining should match. Pin the fabric in place, top and bottom, starting at the positions of the two seam struts.

The outer cover fabric should be a perfect fit, but you will again have to ease it into place, removing any cockling. You can improve the finished product by leaving the lampshade unfinished for a couple of days. Fit the outer cover, pin it into place, and put the shade in the room where it will be used. It will absorb atmospheric moisture, and you may see some slackness appear. You can take up this slackness before finally sewing it in place.

Sew the cover to the top and bottom rings of the frame along the same sewing line as the lining, that is, on the outside edge of the frame. Use small stitches, and be careful not to let the sewing line creep over on to the crest of the binding. Trim the fabric as close to the sewing line as possible. You may find this can be done most easily with sharp nail scissors.

Finishing

There remains only the trim which will give a good border finish to the top and bottom of the shade. Almost any kind of braid or ruche will do the job, or elasticated ribbon, any of them in either a matching or a contrasting colour. You could instead make a trim yourself, the simplest version being one made in the same fabric as the cover itself – 'self-trim'. Cut two strips, each 3 cm wide, one long enough to go round the top ring, the other to fit the bottom ring. They should be cut on the bias for flexibility if you have enough spare fabric. Fold each one into three along its length, like bias binding, and press it.

Measure the circumference of each ring and add a good 5 cm to each length to allow for turnings. Never stretch a trim to fit the frame as it will distort the cover. For this reason be particularly careful when applying elasticated ribbon. Fold under 1 cm at the end of the trimming and starting at one strut pin it on just ahead of your ladder stitching. Keep the stitches as small as possible and do not let them stray into the inside of the shade (fig 1). When you have pinned and sewn all round the ring cut the trimming exactly so that there is 1 cm extra for turning under and abut it with the beginning by

slipstitching the ends together. The joins in the trimming at top and bottom should occur at the same strut.

Velvet ribbon is best glued to the shade since stitching would spoil its effect and the fabric anyway lacks the elasticity required for sewing it on. Gluing is a perfectly feasible alternative for other trims that you might consider sewing on. Apply a thin layer of clear-drying glue to about 15 cm only of the trimming, line it up neatly with the top or bottom of the frame, and press the surfaces together for a short while. Continue gluing round each ring, abutting the turned-under ends as before. Peg the ends together until they have dried thoroughly.

Square shade

The square shade looks relatively simple but requires as much skill in pulling the fabric into shape as for the standard type. A pulled or ruckled panel of fabric will seriously mar its appearance.

Start by binding the frame as before. Then cut four panels of fabric, all of them on the straight grain. Measure the dimensions, and add about 5 cm to the height and width of each panel.

Cut the lining to the same dimensions as the outer fabric. This type of frame is not suitable for a balloon lining, and the outer fabric and lining should be fitted together as a single layer. Machine-sew them together wrong side to wrong side, say 2 cm from the edge and certainly within the area that will be the excess fabric when each panel is fitted to the frame.

Pin each one to the binding, as on the earlier version, and pull and stretch the fabric to a comfortable, taut fit. Start pinning at the centre bottom and pull to the centre top. Draw and ease the fabric down to the two bottom corners in turn, then towards the two top corners. Put in plenty of pins, and be prepared to take them out and re-pin to achieve a good set to the fabric.

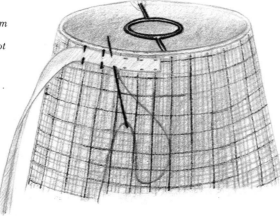

1 *Sew on trimming round the top and bottom of the frame. Keep the stitches small and do not let them stray into the inside of the shade.*

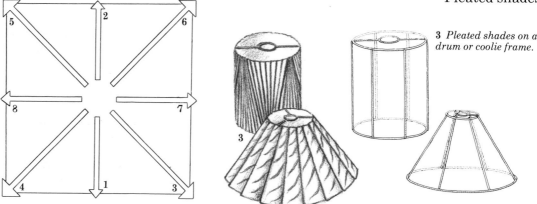

2 *This is the order in which to ease the fabric over the panels of a square-sided frame.*

3 *Pleated shades on a drum or coolie frame.*

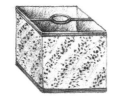

Finally pull the fabric across to the sides. See fig 2 for the order in which to apply the pressure to get the fabric properly fitted.

Sew each panel to the binding with the usual very small stitches, exactly on the crest of the frame. Trim away the excess fabric as close to the new sewing line as you comfortably can without cutting into it.

Complete all four panels. You must now trim the four long edges to conceal the sewing line. Self-trim is good for this purpose (see above), or you could use a braid or manufactured trim if you can find a suitable one. You will need four pieces each long enough for one of the upright struts. First secure the bottom end by sewing it to the binding on the frame. Apply glue in short sections to fix the outer edges of the trim to the cover fabric, or sew the pieces securely to the top of the frame. Do not pull the trim too tight.

Finally, trim the top and bottom of the frame as on the previous shade. Self-trim or any manufactured braid will do the job, attached by either of the methods described.

This is the best method to use for all large lampshades where to handle more than one panel at a time would be unwieldy.

Pleated shades

Among the more elaborate shades, perhaps especially appropriate for bedroom lighting, are shades with pleated covers. Chiffon is particularly recommended but georgette is also suitable. Nylon does not pleat well. This type of shade gives a soft appearance and diffuses light well. Use either a straight-sided drum or a coolie frame (fig 3). The outer cover will be fitted to give a loosely pleated finish, but the lining is fitted smooth.

Bind the frame as before. To fit the lining, measure the frame's circumference and height, and cut the lining to the approximate size of, say, four suitable workable panels. Pin it all round the inside of the bottom of the frame. Arrange the joins to fall at the upright struts, and turn the fabric out towards you as you sew it to the binding so that the cover will later conceal the raw edges. You will have to unpick the seams just enough to pass the lampholder struts, as before.

Cut the chiffon for the outer cover, approximately three times as long as the circumference of the bottom ring, and a good 10 cm wider than the depth of the shade. Cut across the fabric so that the straight grain will run from top to bottom down the shade. Don't worry if you haven't got a suitable complete length of

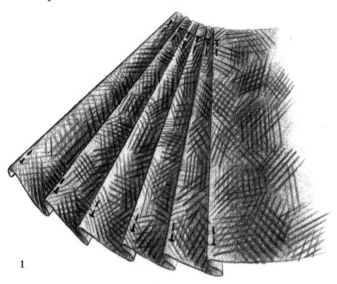

1

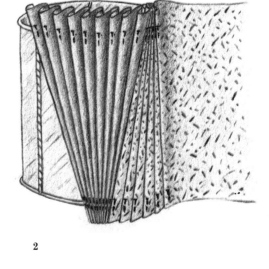

2

1 Pin the pleats to the bottom and top rings. On a coolie or other frame, where the top ring is smaller than the bottom, it is quite tricky keeping the pleats symmetrical.

To add in a new length of fabric invisibly, turn under the previous pleat and slip the new raw edge behind it. Keep the pins facing away from the edges.

2 Fan pleating is only possible on a straight-sided frame. Divide the circumference up into quarters, say, and arrange one upwards and one downwards section in each quarter.

material, but see below for how to deal with joins.

Start at one of the struts and turn under 5 mm along the raw edge. Pin the material to the bottom binding, gathering it into tiny pleats as you go, approximately 1–2 cm all round the frame. This will be easier on a straight drum frame; on a coolie frame the main difficulty in making this type of shade lies in keeping the pleats straight up to the top ring. Use the struts as a guide and work in a symmetrical pattern, vertical at the centres sloping to the sides at the struts, and merging neatly between the two. There must be the same number of pleats between each strut. Join the fabric at the same strut as the lining, again by turning it under, and slipping the other raw edge behind it (fig 1). When the material is pleated satisfactorily top and bottom, sew the fabric to the binding.

If you have to work the shade for more than one length of material, do not sew down the join but merely turn under the new length and position it over the previous raw edge to form the next pleat. When you get back to the beginning, trim the raw edge to the correct length and tuck

it under the fold of the first pleat. Trim close to the stitching before finishing the shade with a suitable braid or fringe as before.

A pretty variation is to pleat round the top ring but gather along the bottom edge. Adjust the gathers evenly before you sew. Another possibility is to plan small gaps between the pleats; or you could tackle fan pleating (only possible on a straight-side frame) by arranging equal alternate sections of pleating as in fig 2.

Tiffany lampshades

These lampshades are popular for many rooms and range from an informal and pretty style in gingham, lawn, other light dress cotton, lace or broderie anglaise, through to a more tailored and luxurious look, perhaps for a formal table lamp, in a heavy silk or Dupion.

There are two construction methods – the gathered tube and the tailored version. The gathered tube is easier and more informal and can have a frill round the bottom edge. Start by preparing and binding the frame as usual. For the gathered style you need only bind the

rings, but the tailored version should be bound on every third strut, dividing the frame into quarters.

For the gathered version, measure round the circumference of the bottom ring and add 10 cm. The width of the material will be the depth of the frame plus about 6 cm. The fabric must be cut so that the straight grain will run down the shade from the top to bottom. If you haven't enough material to cut the piece from a single length, make it up from two equal lengths, so that the seam will fall exactly at a strut.

You will need the same amount of lining fabric. Treat the top and lining fabrics as one by joining them wrong sides together in a French seam (start with the fabrics right sides out so that the seam will end up after the second row of stitching on the wrong side). Press the seam to one side.

At both long edges turn in a double 1.25 cm casing. Leave a 3 or 4 cm gap at the seams for inserting elastic (fig 3). Introduce lengths of string into each casing and try the shade on the frame, adjusting each piece to fit. These will be the lengths of the elastic needed, but add on a centimetre or so to secure the ends.

If you are planning to have a frill at the bottom edge, mark the position of its sewing line while it is on the frame. This will be along the edge of the bottom ring (fig 4).

Insert the elastic into both casings, overlap and secure the ends, and close the gaps in the casings by hemming.

The frill should also be cut on the straight grain. It should be 10–15 cm wide and 1½ times the length of the circumference of the bottom ring. Join the two short ends in a narrow French seam. Fold the material in two lengthwise, right sides out. Turn under the raw edges just over 1 cm at the top. Gather within that margin through the layers. Draw up the gathers evenly, pin the frill to the fitting line and sew it neatly to the cover (fig 5).

3

4

5

3 *Treat the top and lining fabrics as one. At both long edges turn in a double 1.25 cm casing, leaving short gaps in which to insert elastic.*

4 *If you want to have a frill at the bottom instead of elastic, mark the position along the bottom ring while the cover is on the frame.*

5 *When the frill is attached, draw up the gathers evenly, and pin and sew the frill to the fitting line.*

Lampshades

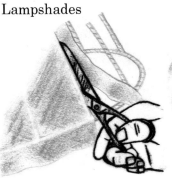 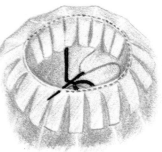 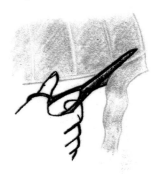 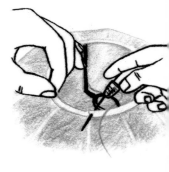

1 *Tiffany lampshade. On the outside of the frame oversew each panel to the binding along all edges. Trim one side close to the strut. Fit the next panel at this edge.*

2 *Fit the main fabric similarly. Trim excess fabric top and bottom close to the rings but leave excess lining. Cut*

slits in the lining down to the rings, turn them down and sew to the binding low down on the ring.

3 *Trim the surplus fabric.*

4 *Attach trim round the top ring by stab-stitching through the binding.*

Tailored tiffany lampshade

The work involved in making a tailored tiffany shade is much more like that for the standard shade described first in this chapter, except that it is made in four sections, each one covering three panels. Do not choose a frame that is too sloping at top or bottom.

Both the lining and the top material should be cut on the bias in order to get a better fit. You may find it easiest to make a paper pattern which you can then arrange on the fabric in order to find out how much to buy. Remember to allow more for matching strongly patterned fabrics or particular central motifs.

Deal with the lining first – it is fitted to the outside of the frame. Pin it to the outer strut and along the rings, easing and adjusting as usual. Trim the excess material to 1.5 cm at the struts and 2.5 cm at top and bottom. Oversew the lining to the binding along all the edges. Then trim one side, probably the right-hand one, close to the strut (fig 1). Start fitting the next panel at this trimmed edge.

When you have lined the shade, deal with the main cover in the same way, but trim the excess fabric close to the rings as well as the struts. Cut slits in the lining down to the top ring so that it can turn over the top. Sew low down round the ring, and trim the surplus (figs 2 & 3). Repeat for the bottom ring.

Glue self-trim or other suitable braid down the seamed struts in order to cover the stitching, as explained on page 116. Also attach some of the trim round the top ring by stab-stitching over and under the ring (fig 4), abutting the ends. Glue fringing or braid round the bottom ring.

Handkerchief lampshade

Another pretty and extremely simple design for a lampshade is the handkerchief lampshade. You will need a utility ring and a square metre of fabric. Cotton or lawn would be a good choice of fabric, or any other similarly translucent material. Sew round the square in a double hem turned to the wrong side, or make a scalloped edge with machine zigzagging, trimming the edge after sewing. You may find it easiest to use sharp nail scissors for the job.

Fold the fabric in four to find the centre, mark it, and cut a hole just large enough so that the flex from the ceiling can pass through it. Bind round the hole with hand overcasting or machine zigzagging, or use bias binding.

Feed the flex through the hole, connect the utility ring, the lightbulb holder and the bulb.

Firm lampshades

The principles involved in making firm lampshades are not greatly different from those applied to soft fabric shades, but paper covers offer a greater scope for creative variations, such as attaching pressed dried flowers or appliqué work or individual motifs to one or more of the panels, painting the panels, and so on.

As well as the usual equipment for the other type of lampshade-making, you will need a ring set – two rings for the top and bottom of the shade, one attached to the appropriate lampholder fitting whether gimbal or pendant – a metal ruler, clear-setting glue and hinged wooden clothes ·pegs. A strutted frame can also be used for a base.

Firm lampshades do not need a lining. The choice of material used for the cover is not wide: real parchment is the traditional material, but buckram is much more usual, and very much cheaper. Buckram, particularly the rough-

looking brown sort used for pelmets, can stand effectively on its own, or be painted, or used as a backing for a soft fabric such as cotton, lace or even embroidered panels. Hand-painting on a panel of pale buckram would show off an additional accomplishment. A limited range of lampshade parchments with fabric already attached is available in large stores, and covered lampshade card too. For the rest of this chapter we will refer only to buckram.

The easiest shape to deal with is a not-too-large straight-sided drum. The rings in the set should be the same size as each other. You need buckram the height of the finished shade (plus about 5 cm) by the circumference of the rings (plus 2 cm or so). It is wise to make a paper pattern (though not essential for this shape if you are confident) so that you can assess the proportions – any fabric cover for the buckram can also be cut from it. The pattern must be cut with the corners square to ensure the accuracy of the cover.

Bind each ring as usual. If you are covering a strutted frame you don't need to bind the struts. If you are attaching fabric to the buckram, do so before you cut out the rectangle. Wipe over its smooth side with a damp sponge before pressing on the fabric (right side out) with a hot iron. Cover the fabric with a damp cloth and iron the bonded material again.

There are two methods for attaching the buckram to the shade. The first is to apply a thin layer of glue round the outside of one of the rings. Peg the cover to it so that the edge of the paper extends beyond the ring by ·a bare 5 mm. Leave the excess for the overlapped seam down the side unglued. Treat the other ring in the same way. Adjust the side seam allowance by trimming it to an exact 5 mm, and glue the join (fig 5). When the glue has dried, stitch along the top and bottom to attach the cover to the binding. Use double thread, and make small stitches inside the drum (fig 6). You can make

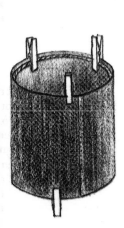

5 *Glue round the rings in turn and peg the paper to extend to 5 mm beyond the ring set. Glue down the vertical join.*

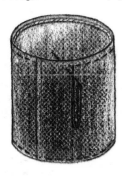

6 *When the glue has dried stitch the paper to the binding making small stitches with double thread.*

7 *Otherwise you can use blanket-stitch to attach the paper to the bound rings.*

Lampshades

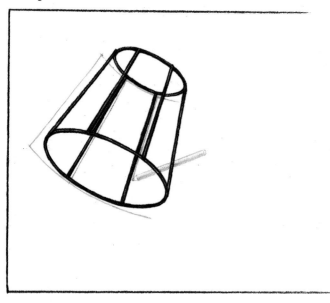

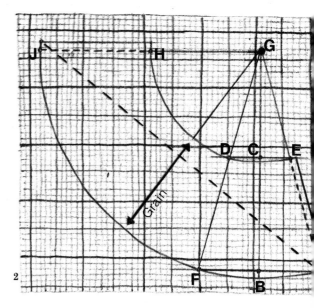

1 Make a paper pattern for any strutted frame other than a straight drum by rotating the frame and marking its dimensions on stiff paper.

2 For a ring set mark the dimensions you want on graph paper as explained in the right-hand column.

them slightly longer on the outside where they will be covered by braid. Gluing on the braid or other trimming is the final stage of the construction. The abutted ends top and bottom should be at the same side of the frame.

The other method dispenses with glue except for the side seam and for attaching the trim. The top and bottom edges of the shade must be trimmed flush to the outer edges of the rings. Blanket-stitch through the buckram round the rings as in fig 7 on page 121, stopping short of the side seam by 5 cm. Mark with a light pencil on the wrong side of the buckram the exact vertical to form a neat overlap. Glue it down, and resume the blanket-stitching to close the gaps top and bottom. Glue the braid or trimming round the rings, covering the blanket-stitching.

You don't have to make a paper pattern if you are making a drum-shaped shade, but it is necessary for any other shape such as a cone or straight-sided empire shade.

Bind the rings or frame as usual. For a strutted frame, take a large piece of stiff paper. Mark down one of the side struts with pencil. Gradu-

ally turn the frame, marking the curve formed by the two rings and also the position of each strut until you arrive back at the beginning. Add on 1.5 cm for a seam allowance (fig 1). Don't waver as you rotate the frame.

If the frame is very large make a pattern of half of it, and cut two pieces with it, one in reverse of the other. Fit the pattern to the frame to make any adjustments before you cut out the buckram.

For a ring set, you will need some graph paper. Measure the eventual height of the shade and the diameter and circumference of each of the rings. From the corner of the graph paper at **A**, plot the diameter of the bottom ring to **F**. From the middle point of that line (**B**) take up a vertical the length of the height of the shade. Draw another horizontal line through that point (**C**) the length of the diameter of the top ring. Join up the ends of the two horizontal lines which will give you a shape resembling the frame itself (**FDEA**). Continue them until they meet. Use that junction (**G**) as a pivotal point: fix a pencil to a piece of string the exact length of **GE**. Tether the loose end of the string to **G** with a

122

drawing-pin. Draw an arc from **E** round to **H**, the arc being the circumference of the top ring. Perform a similar operation with another piece of string the exact length of **GA**, taking the pencil round to **J**. That arc will be the circumference of the bottom ring.

You will now have the exact size of the shade (**JHEA**) but add on about 5 mm to one edge to form an overlap. A line drawn through **JH** should arrive at **G** if you have plotted the measurements accurately. The grain line guide for the fabric will divide the wedge in two. Cut out the pattern and try it by pegging it on the rings. When you arrive at a satisfactory fit proceed as explained earlier for the drum shade.

Care of lampshades

If you plan to wash the lampshade, bear this in mind from the planning stages and choose colourfast fabric, lining and trimming. The shade must dry as quickly as possible to prevent the frame rusting. Use a mild detergent, rinse the shade thoroughly in warm water and dry it in the sun. A spell afterwards in an airing cupboard or other warm spot will help the fabric to tauten on the frame.

Firm shades and non-washable fabrics should be kept clean by regular soft brushing. Scotchguard produces an aerosol for protecting clothes which can also be sprayed on a finished lampshade to protect it from spots and stains.

Table linen

This section contains some of the quickest, easiest and cheapest projects in the book that also lend themselves to great adaptation and variation. For instance, you could make several tablecloths of different lengths and edgings for different occasions, with matching or contrasting mats, coasters and napkins.

Reversible quilting is particularly suitable for mats and tea cosies, and for the top of the round gathered tablecloth, because of its insulating qualities. Polyester-cotton mixtures are good for cloths and napkins, and cotton seersucker needs little ironing. Some loose-weave materials are also appropriate for cloths but above all the fabrics used in this section should be washable, colourfast and easily ironed.

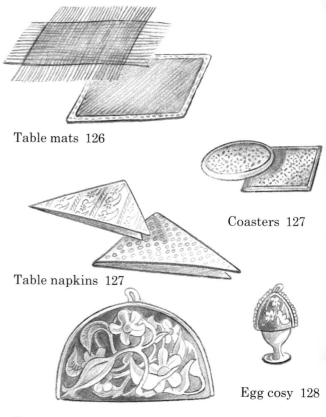

Square or rectangular tablecloth

You may already have a tablecloth that fits your table which you can use as a guide to find out how much material to buy. Otherwise, decide whether you want the cloth to be floor-length (the table's legs may be unsightly), lap-length or even shorter if it is to be an over-cloth. Do the measuring with a fabric tape measure. If the cloth is to be lap-length, sit at the table to gauge the level correctly. Add on enough for double hems – double 2.5 cm would be appropriate for heavier fabrics, while light fabrics would need only double 1.25 cm ones. All corners should be mitred. Machine-sew round the hems, or hand-sew them for a better finish.

Many of the fabrics suitable for table linen come in very wide widths, but if you do need to join widths to make up the total requirement, let the seams fall equally to the sides of the cloth, never down the centre. Use run-and-fell seams to neaten all the raw edges.

Round tablecloth

Measure the table's diameter and the margin of overhang that you want. If you are making a floor-length tablecloth, allow for it just to clear the floor. To the table top's diameter, add on twice the height of the overhang, plus 6 cm for two double 1.5 cm hems.

With run-and-fell seams, join widths of fabric as necessary on each side of the main part in order to make up just over the approximate measurement you want. Fold the material in half right sides together so that the seams coincide, and fold in the other direction so that you get a rough square. Attach a piece of string to dressmaker's chalk or an ordinary pencil and pin the other end of the string through the corner where all the folds meet, such that the length of string is half the total diameter of the cloth.

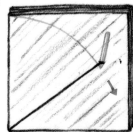

For a round cloth mark a circle for cutting by folding the fabric in half and half again, then anchoring at the centre point a piece of string of the required radius attached at the other end to a pencil, and drawing round the arc of the quarter-circle.

Draw round the arc of the quarter-circle, and cut round the mark. Turn in a double 1.5 cm hem, and sew it with two rows of stitching. The first row will close the hem and you will have to ease the fullness in the fabric by snipping into the allowance. The second row should be close to the fold to define clearly the edge of tablecloth.

Fitted round tablecloth

A more complicated type of round tablecloth has a flat top with a gathered overhang usually descending right to the floor. Cut the top to the same surface area as the table allowing for a 1.5 cm seam allowance all round. Lay it on the table and weight it so that it does not move. Then mark with pins all round the line of the table's edge. You could sew piping round the seam if you wanted.

The overhang is made in the form of a skirt, cut as a rectangle of cloth measuring up to twice the circumference of the circle. You could make it $1\frac{1}{2}$ times the circumference but the skirt will hang more skimpily.

The width will be the depth of the overhang plus 1.25 cm for the seam at the top and 5 cm for a double 2.5 cm hem at the bottom. On a floor-length tablecloth the skirt should fall from the top of the table to the point just clearing the floor. Join the two ends of the skirt into a continuous circle. Turn up and hand-sew the double hem, checking that any pattern is upright.

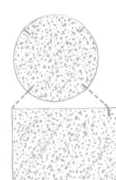

1 *For a fitted round cloth, divide both the skirt and the top circle into quarters. Gather up each skirt quarter to fit a top quarter.*

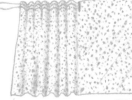

Divide both the length of the skirt, and the circumference of the circle, into four equal parts, marking them with pins. Gather up the skirt with two rows of thread about 5 mm apart, working to the quarter-circumference measurement in order to gather an even skirt all round (fig 1). Otherwise, it is easy to be left with too much fullness at one side and too little at the other.

Machine-sew the skirt to the top seam allowance (1.5 cm) with at least two rows of stitching for strength.

Scalloped edging

If your sewing-machine has a zigzag facility, satin-stitching sewn in scallop shapes can look attractive to edge the bottom of a tablecloth, round or square. Measure and cut the fabric, and with dressmaker's chalk draw round the edge of a saucer or wineglass to form a series of arcs (fig 2).

Zigzag stitch all round in a similar or contrasting colour. Trim off the excess cloth without cutting the thread – you may find nail scissors the best tool for the job. You could also follow shapes in the fabric itself to produce an irregular scalloped effect.

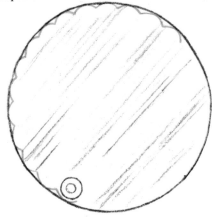

2 *Make a scalloped edge by drawing round a saucer or wine glass to form a series of arcs.*

Table mats

You can set a table mat on a tablecloth or use it directly on the table as a protection for the furniture. Do not rely on anything other than quilted fabric or fabric backed with terylene wadding to shield the table from hot plates. Whatever you use should be washable and colourfast.

Start with a rectangle of fabric about 23 × 30 cm – this is a useful size because you can cut four pieces from a single width of 120 cm fabric.

You could hand-sew a simple double hem all round, or add a braid or bias edging. You could also sew a double line of stitches 1 or 2 cm from each edge to fix the fabric, and with a needle carefully pull away the threads outside the stitches to form a fringe (fig 3). You could also

To make a fringed edging for table mats, coasters or napkins, fix the fabric with a double line of stitching a couple of centimetres in from the edge. Then with a needle pull the threads beyond the stitching to form a fringe.

use the zigzag stitch on your sewing-machine, perhaps using an interesting colour for the thread to echo the scalloped edging on a tablecloth (see earlier in the chapter).

Patchwork, quilting (page 136), appliqué work and embroidery can all be brought into play in the making of attractive table mats.

Coasters

As with table mats, coasters can be vehicles to show off other decorative skills while protecting the table top from hot or sticky liquids. They can be square or circular – sides or a diameter of about 10 cm would be an appropriate size. Give square coasters fringed or hemmed and mitred edges. Don't use thick braid as the added level may cause a carelessly placed glass to tip over. To get an accurate circle for a round coaster, either draw round an object of a suitable size or adapt the principle outlined on page 125.

Table napkins

Table napkins are generally square – sides of 50 cm will be generous. A narrow double 5 mm hem in conjunction with mitred corners produces the neatest finish, but you could give the napkin a contrasting hem in the form of bias binding sewn over the raw edge of the main fabric, or follow the scalloped edge theme (see above).

A matching square, probably smaller than the napkin but with similar edging, would make an attractive lining for a round bread basket.

Tea cosy

The most usual type of tea cosy consists of an inner and an outer cover with wadding between the layers to give the necessary insulation.

Take two roughly semi-circular pieces of easily washable cotton for the inner lining and pin them to fit comfortably over the tea-pot's spout and handle. Try them on the tea-pot before you cut round the shape. There should be enough material for turning up a small bottom hem at a later stage. Right sides together, sew a seam round the pin line. Trim the seam. Lay the inner cover on the outer fabric. Cut two pieces for the outer cover, 1.5 cm larger than the finished lining, with a 1.5 cm seam allowance all round.

Before sewing the cover, prepare a length of piping to run the length of the seam. Also make a loop, if you want to hang up the tea cosy, in the same fabric as the piping casing. Cut a piece of fabric 15 cm by 6 cm. Fold in the two long sides, right sides out, and then fold the strip over again. Slipstitch the long edges together. Pin the loop halfway along the tea cosy, and with right sides together and enclosing the piping, sew the main seam (fig 1 overleaf).

Cut two sheets of terylene wadding for the insulating layer. Cut them slightly smaller than the lining, and catchstitch the edges to its seam allowance (fig 2 overleaf). Slip the outer cover over the whole assembly and turn in the hems of both the inner and outer covers. Machine-stitch or slip-stitch them together by hand. You could enclose the finished bottom edge with binding in the same fabric as the piping casing.

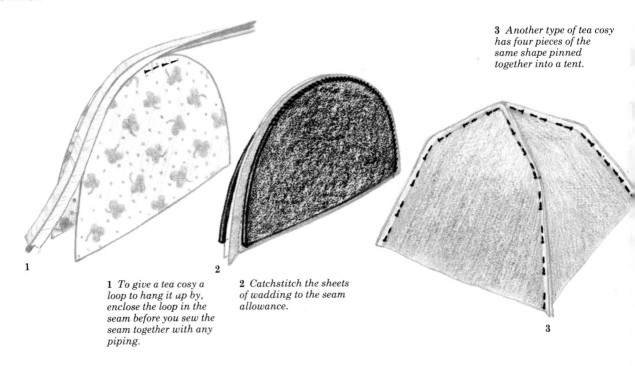

3 *Another type of tea cosy has four pieces of the same shape pinned together into a tent.*

1 *To give a tea cosy a loop to hang it up by, enclose the loop in the seam before you sew the seam together with any piping.*

2 *Catchstitch the sheets of wadding to the seam allowance.*

As a variation, try the four-cornered tea cosy. Again, it is wise to pin first to get the right shape before you cut any fabric. The idea on this cover is to taper the corners of four squares of fabric to a point at the centre top.

Pin the four pieces into a kind of tent (fig 3). When you have arrived at the best size and fit, use one piece as a template for the wadding, which should be very slightly smaller than the lining, and for the outer cover pieces – these should be larger than the lining by 1.5 cm at each seam. Sew the lining pieces together and then the outer cover pieces, inserting the loop at the top and the piping down all the seams. Invert the outer cover only.

Catchstitch the nylon wadding to the seam allowances of the lining to hold it in place. Slip the outer cover over the lining. Machine-stitch or hand-sew round the bottom seam, or enclose it with binding to match the piping casing.

The simplest method of all is to use reversible quilted fabric cut to two semi-circles just larger than the tea-pot, and sewn together with or without piping or a hanging loop. Neaten the bottom edge with bias binding.

Egg cosy

Adapt the last method suggested for making a tea cosy, scaled down to size. Egg cosies are sometimes made in felt and can be decorated with felt appliqué work.

Conversion chart

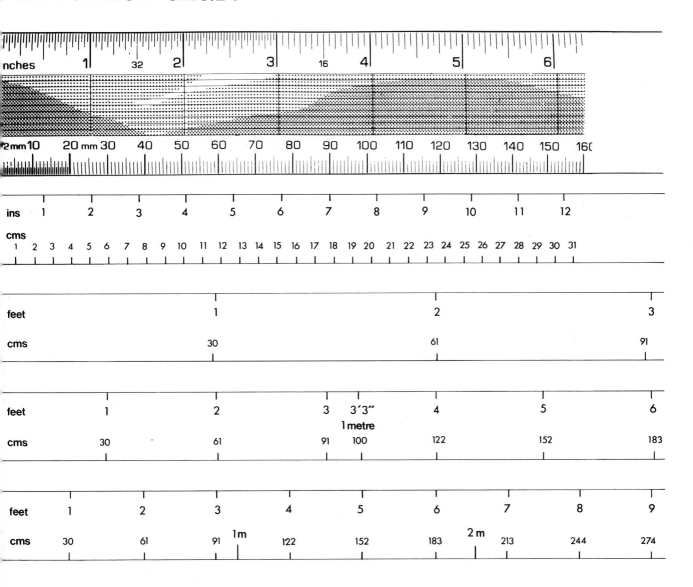

nches 1 32 2 3 16 4 5 6

2mm 10 20 mm 30 40 50 60 70 80 90 100 110 120 130 140 150 160

ins 1 2 3 4 5 6 7 8 9 10 11 12

cms 1 2 3 4 5 6 7 8 9 10 11 12 13 14 15 16 17 18 19 20 21 22 23 24 25 26 27 28 29 30 31

feet 1 2 3

cms 30 61 91

feet 1 2 3 3′3″ 4 5 6
1 metre
cms 30 61 91 100 122 152 183

feet 1 2 3 4 5 6 7 8 9

cms 30 61 91 1m 122 152 183 2m 213 244 274

Basic sewing techniques

The sewing skills required in soft furnishing are few. Anyone with a basic grounding in sewing should be able to master them and someone who has tackled the far more intricate work of dressmaking will find soft furnishing relatively easy.

Stitches

Tacking

This is a quick temporary stitch for holding together two or more pieces of fabric before the final stitching is put in. It is sometimes used to hold hems and seams in place before they are machine-sewn or more finely finished by hand, but can often be omitted if the fitting and pinning stages are carefully done.

Cut a short length of thread (40–50 cm) and make a small backstitch at the start of the line for tacking. (Don't cut off too long a length as it will get easily knotted.) Sew through both or all pieces of fabric, going from right to left along the line where the final stitching is to be. Push the needle down through the fabric and back towards you in a single movement, forming stitches about a centimetre long. Pull the needle back out of the fabric until the thread is taut, but don't pull the fabric out of shape. Take the needle along another centimetre to repeat the stitch. At the end of the tacking line, sew a couple of times through the fabric, and break or cut the thread. When you have completed your final sewing you can cut the tacking at any point and pull it out from the end, leaving no trace.

An alternative to this is the quicker *uneven tacking*, particularly useful in curtain-making where large expanses of material are being dealt with. For the first stitch, take the needle along 2 cm, form a stitch about 5 mm long, then move along another 2 cm to repeat the stitch.

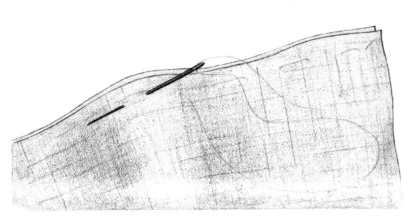

Tacking

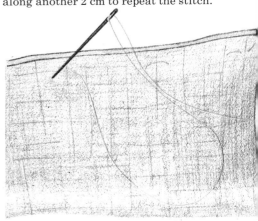

Uneven tacking

Slipstitch

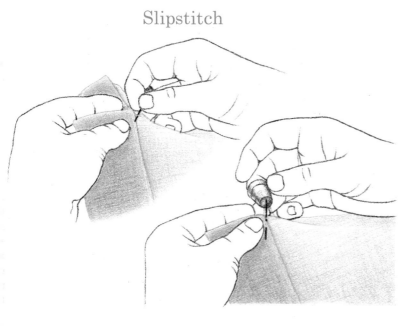

about 1 cm – or less if you find that more manageable. In the same movement bring the needle out through the edge of the hem, and pull the stitch taut but not tight. Follow the same sequence: pick up two threads of the facing fabric, insert the needle into the edge of the hem exactly opposite the last part of the stitch, and go along inside the hem for another 1 cm.

On the facing side of the fabric you will see nothing more than a neat line of points, and maybe not even that if your thread is close enough in colour to the fabric.

When joining two folds of fabric, as in a mitred corner, insert the needle into the fold at the point exactly opposite, then let it emerge about 6 or 7 mm along.

Hem stitch

This serves the same purpose as slipstitching when a fold is to be joined to a flat area of fabric and can be as nearly invisible on the right side if carefully done. It is not so neat as slipstitch on the wrong side but it is probably a little easier. Secure the thread at the beginning of the hem. Sew from right to left, pick up a couple of threads from the wrong side of the flat piece of fabric, and in the same movement pick up a small amount through both layers of the hem. The needle should point diagonally right to left as in the drawing. Pull the needle through to draw up the thread.

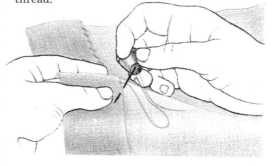

This stitch is used extensively in sewing the side and bottom hems in curtains, and in other situations where the aim is to achieve neat stitching with hardly any marks showing on the facing side of the fabric. It is also used to join two folds of fabric, as in mitred corners (page 135).

To join a folded edge to a flat piece of material, as in a hem, have the fabric wrong side up, with the pinned hem ready for sewing towards you. Hold the beginning of the hem under your thumb and second finger, anchored underneath by your third finger. Sew from right to left. Start by making a small knot or two small stitches in the hem turning. Bring the needle out through the fold of the hem, and pick up two strands of the facing fabric on its wrong side. Do this carefully and neatly because it will show as a small point on the facing side when the article is finished. The points should be small and evenly spaced. Insert the needle into the hem exactly opposite the stitch, and run it along inside the hem for

Running (gathering) stitch

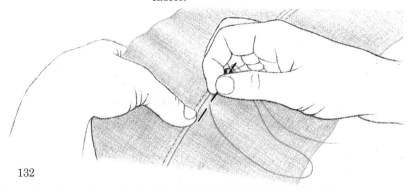

A running or gathering stitch is often used, as its name suggests, for preparing material which is to be gathered up. Usually two parallel rows are made, about 2 mm apart, for strength. You can work on the right or the wrong side of the fabric. Start with a knot or double stitch and weave the needle in and out of the fabric several times before pulling the needle through. Each stitch should be no more than 2 mm long.

Backstitch

This is the hand-sewn equivalent of machine-stitching. In soft furnishing it is used for sewing zips in loose covers as it is very strong. It is also useful for when the machine cannot cope with the bulk of material.

Start with a small knot or double stitch. Sew through from front to back and along 5 mm, bringing the needle through to the front, all in one movement. Pull the needle through to tauten the thread. Go back 2.5 mm. Push the needle through to the back and along another 5 mm. You will find that you are sewing a continuous line of thread on both the front and back of the fabric.

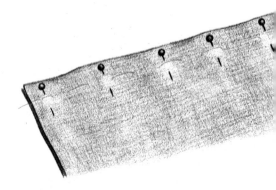

Seams

Simple flat seam

This seam, used for joining fabric widths, consists of a single line of sewing far enough from the edges to avoid fraying. Pin the two fabrics edge to edge, right sides together. If you like, tack along a line about 1.5 cm from the edges, then sew along the same line, securing the seam ends with a couple of backstitches. Open out the fabric, wrong sides up. Separate the seam turnings and press them flat, unless there are instructions to the contrary.

It is wise to neaten a simple seam to prevent the raw edges fraying. You can do this by following the method on page 31 (best if one of the pieces of fabric is gathered), or by over-casting or pinking.

To overcast, work from left to right, bringing the needle through from behind the work at quite an acute angle. You can sew the two halves of the seam individually, or together if there won't be a problem of bulk.

To pink the edges, machine-sew along each seam-half 5 mm from the raw edges, before cutting along with pinking shears.

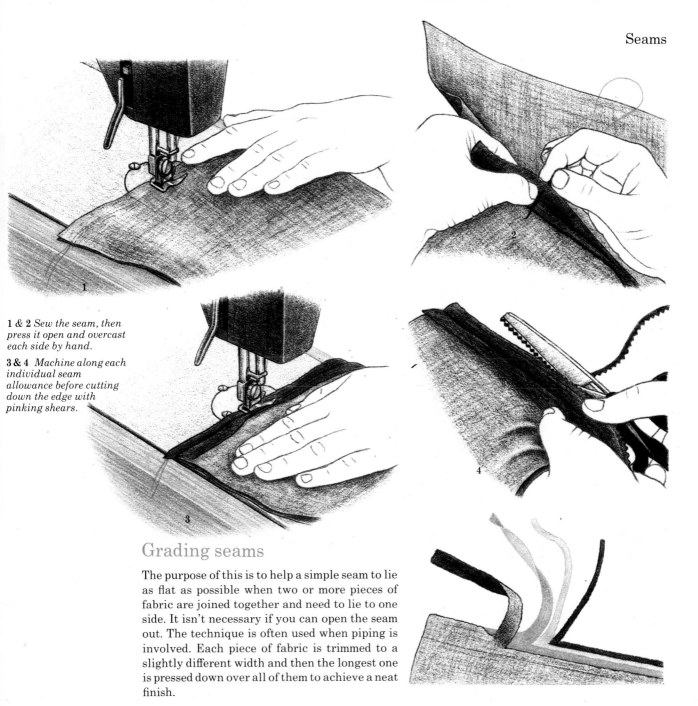

1 & 2 *Sew the seam, then press it open and overcast each side by hand.*

3 & 4 *Machine along each individual seam allowance before cutting down the edge with pinking shears.*

Grading seams

The purpose of this is to help a simple seam to lie as flat as possible when two or more pieces of fabric are joined together and need to lie to one side. It isn't necessary if you can open the seam out. The technique is often used when piping is involved. Each piece of fabric is trimmed to a slightly different width and then the longest one is pressed down over all of them to achieve a neat finish.

French seam

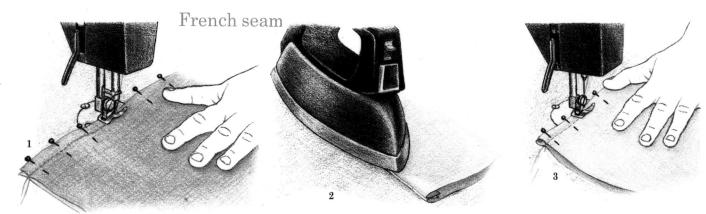

1, 2 & 3 French seam. Sew the two pieces of fabric right sides out. Press the seam so that the turnings are to the inside and the stitching line occurs at the fold. Sew again to enclose the first seam which will be on the wrong side.

This seam does not need to be neatened since it encloses the raw edges within itself, avoiding the problems of fraying. It can be used whenever the wrong side of the seam is left unconcealed, for example on net curtains or unlined curtains, but is too bulky for heavy fabrics.

Lay the fabrics edge to edge, wrong sides together. Pin and sew along the length 1 cm in from the edges, securing the ends of the thread with a couple of backstitches. Trim that seam allowance to 5 mm. Turn the fabrics the other way round, right sides together, and adjust them so that the sewing line is right on the edge. It may help to press the seam. Sew a second line, exactly 1 cm from the new edge. Open out the fabric. You will have a small pocket standing out from the wrong side of the fabric: the pocket itself is finished with a line of sewing, the raw edges tucked inside the pocket where they cannot fray. The double line of stitching gives additional strength to the seam. Press the pocket down to one side.

Run-and-fell seam

A run-and-fell seam has similar advantages but secures the pocket to the wrong side of the curtain. It is useful for nets or other transparent fabric where any seams can be seen from the right side and it is also very strong with well-enclosed raw edges.

Pin the two pieces right sides together. Sew by hand or machine along a line 1.5 cm in from the edges. Press the turnings to one side. Then trim the lower one to a width of 7.5 mm. Fold the longer allowance under the shorter one, and press it to a neat line. Sew it to the wrong side of the curtain along its length. You could machine-sew it but if you don't want the seam to show it is best to slipstitch the allowance to the fabric.

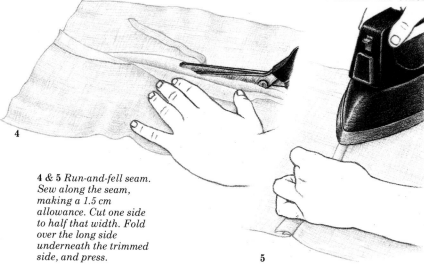

4 & 5 Run-and-fell seam. Sew along the seam, making a 1.5 cm allowance. Cut one side to half that width. Fold over the long side underneath the trimmed side, and press.

Clipping curves and corners

Mitring corners

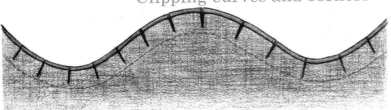

Clipping curves is done to enable fabric to lie flat when the stitching would otherwise pull it out of shape. Gentle curves do not need so many notches as sharp ones. Clipping corners helps to reduce bulk when the corner is turned to the inside.

Mitring is a method of neatening a corner and is commonly used in the making of curtains and bedspreads. Turn the raw edges at the corner in by 5 mm, and press them. Then turn the edges over again so that these new folds are where you want the edge of the hem to be. Press them lightly. Open out the last folds and turn up the corner. Trim across the corner to 5 mm. Then fold back the double hem with the two diagonal edges abutting neatly, and slipstitch them together.

Mitring corners
6 *Press in the raw edges at the corner.*
7 *Press in again by the depth of the hem.*
8 *Open out the folds to reveal the corner.*
9 *Fold in the corner; press it.*
10 *Trim it across.*
11 *Fold back along the creases; slipstitch the diagonal edges together.*

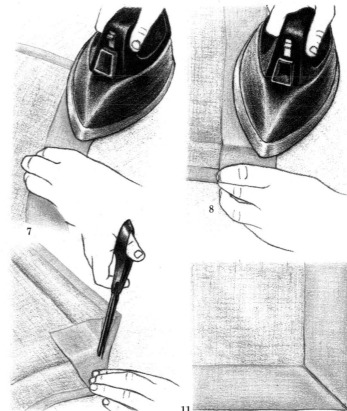

Quilting

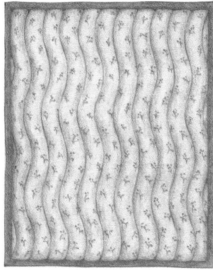

1

2

3

1 & 2 Simple all-over machine-quilted designs.

3 A central area can be given an elaborate design with the rest of the quilt left plain as a foil. The design shown is worked in trapunto and Italian quilting.

Quilting is one of the oldest of household crafts. It probably originated in Europe in the 11th and 12th centuries. In its simplest form, it is a method of holding two layers of fabric together with a layer of insulation between them for warmth. Traditionally, almost any form of filling was used, from wool left by sheep on hedgerows and fences to shreds of old material. Quilting came to be widely practised and different regions developed their own traditional patterns. With its close cousin, patchwork, it soon attained the level of a craft, examples of which may be seen in museums around the world.

If you set out to make a quilted object, whether or not with patchwork, choose the simplest design in order to show off the work to best effect. Examples might be the square cushion (page 93), the throw-over bedspread (page 50) or the most straightforward of the designs for tea cosies (page 128).

It is usual to use terylene wadding as the filling, though bump and domette are possible choices, or even an old blanket. Synthetic wadding is available in several thicknesses appropriate to its intended use.

The best fabrics to use for quilting are natural ones. Synthetic fabrics are more resistant to shaping. Satin and sateen with their sheen are good for showing off the pattern, and velvet, silk and fine wool will also produce a luxurious item. You can have a backing of calico, sheeting or muslin, or use the main fabric on both sides so that the quilt is reversible.

When machine-sewing the quilt, the stitches can go through all three layers, but if you are making a quilted bedcover you will almost certainly be unable to get the work under the machine arm, so you will either have to work by hand, or deal with the quilt in sections, making the joins part of the overall design.

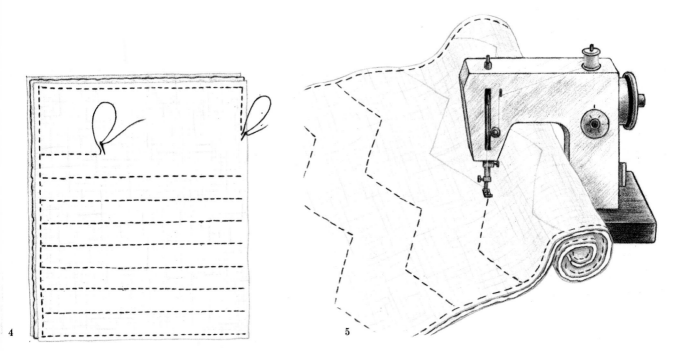

4 *Tack the top fabric, wadding and backing fabric together through all layers across the width of the quilt and all the way round the edge.*

5 *For a straightforward design sewn by machine, keep the finished part of the quilt well rolled up under the machine arm.*

The design will be either a simple arrangement of stitches or a series of more or less elaborate repeats of a pattern (figs 1 & 2). It is not necessary to cover the whole area with an elaborate design – you could work just the central part or even one corner. The remainder should be quilted with a simple all-over pattern of squared, rectangular or diamond stitches (fig 3).

Cut out the fabric for the top and the backing. They may be the same for a reversible article. For the underside of a bedcover, you will probably want to use a fabric which isn't shiny so that the quilt won't slip off the bed. Add 7.5 cm to the length and width to give 2.5 cm turnings all round and to allow for the slight reduction in size caused by the quilting.

Cut the wadding to the same size as the outer fabrics: if you have to join widths, overlap the edges of the wadding, and secure them with a large running stitch.

Plan the design, deciding if necessary where the separate sections will be so that the seams can form part of the pattern. Mark the pattern for the quilting on the top fabric. Sketch or trace the design on to tracing paper, and tack along the lines of the pattern. Tear away the tracing paper, leaving the design in tacking on the top fabric. You could instead trace on a design using dressmaker's carbon paper. If you want to copy an interesting pattern taken from a book, cut a template in cardboard, and draw round it with tailor's chalk.

Place the three layers of fabric together, the two outer fabrics with the wadding between them. Run a line of tacking stitches from side to side across the centre of the article and other lines parallel to it every 5 cm or so, covering the whole quilt, and also tack round the edges. This will prevent the work slipping about and causing puckering (fig 4).

Basic sewing techniques

1 & 2 *Joining quilted sections. Fold under the seam allowance of one section and trim its wadding level with the new edge. On the next section trim the wadding to the same depth but don't fold in the seam allowance. Instead, sandwich the raw edges between the first section's folds.*

3 *Strengthen the hem with a double stitching line.*

4 *Bind the edges in the doubled band of fabric and sew twice round for strength.*

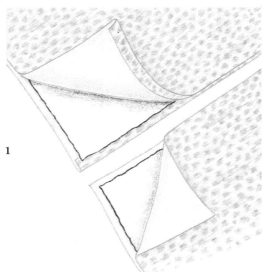

1

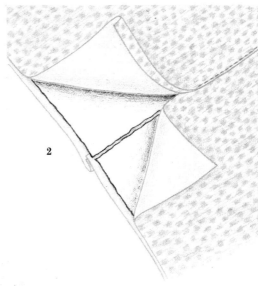

2

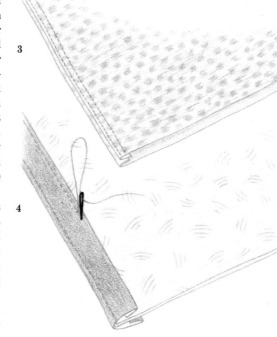

3

4

With the whole assembly fixed in place, you can start working on the design itself. Work from the centre outwards, sewing along the tacking or carbon paper markings. Keep the work as level and even as possible to avoid rucking. Sew either by hand with an even running stitch or back-stitch, or by machine if you can get the work under the machine arm (fig 5 on page 137). If you are working a small item by hand, you can get the best results using an embroidery frame. When you have worked all round the design, sew the fixing stitches over the rest of the area. If you are machine-stitching, use a gauge to ensure that the sewing lines are accurately spaced.

If you have been working in sections, now is the time to join them together. Trim any excess fabric to within about 5 mm of the finished dimensions. Fold in the turnings of one section by 5 mm, and trim away the wadding so that it is level with the turned-in edges. Trim the wadding on the next section to the same level but do not fold in the turnings. Instead, place them between the folded edges of the first section so that the

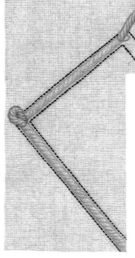

5 *Italian quilting Thread quilting wool through the prepared channel, bringing the needle out at corners or sharp curves. Reintroduce the yarn leaving a small loop.*

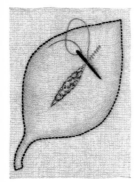

6 *Trapunto quilting. When you have sewn round the design, cut a slit through the backing fabric, pad the area with kapok, and close the slit.*

two pieces of wadding abut (figs 1 & 2). Tack through all the layers and then topstitch along the edge of the folds.

To finish the outer edges, turn the two pieces of fabric in towards each other and secure them with a line of running stitches all round. A second line of stitches half a centimetre in from the edge will help to strengthen the hem (fig 3). Alternatively, you can insert a length of piping or frill between the two outer fabrics. A third method is to bind the edges with a length of matching or contrasting fabric. Press in the edges of the binding, fold the fabric in two lengthwise, and sew it on all round the outside with a double line of stitches for security (fig 4).

Remove the tacking stitches from the quilting. The work should now show up the intended pattern in a form of low relief. This type of quilting is known as *English quilting*.

Italian quilting is purely decorative and does not provide an extra layer of warmth since it has no inner wadding. Two rows of parallel stitching about 5 mm apart are made round the design – often leaves, flowers or scrolls. These form a casing through which is threaded thick yarn or quilting wool to produce a raised effect. It is usual to use a fabric with a sheen which enhances the way the fabric rises and falls, but you can also work with transparent fabrics such as georgette and jap silk and thread different coloured silks through the casings (this is known as *shadow quilting*). You will need backing fabric, probably muslin or calico.

As with English quilting, transfer your design on to the right side of the main fabric, using tracing paper and tacking stitches, or dress-

maker's carbon paper. The finished design will look the most attractive if it is not too dense or complex. Tack the two fabrics together with parallel lines of stitching the length of the material, and tack all round the edges. Hand-sew two parallel lines of stitching round the design using running stitch or backstitch; machine stitching would be a perfectly feasible alternative. Thread a bodkin or blunt tapestry needle with quilting wool and from the back of the work introduce it into one of the channels between the muslin and the top fabric. Where you come to a sharp corner or curve bring the needle out again, always at the back of the work, and reintroduce it at the new angle through the same hole, so that there is a continuous raised line. Leave a small loop of wool at such places. This prevents the work from puckering (fig 5).

Trapunto quilting is really a cross between English and Italian quilting in that single lines of stitching are made round the design, and then wadding is stuffed between the two layers of fabric to make large raised areas. You can use kapok, cotton wool or synthetic fibre as the padding.

Follow the same order for the other types of quilting: transfer the design on to the main fabric, tack the muslin and the main fabric together with rows of parallel stitching the length of the work and all round the edge; then sew round the design on the machine or by hand using running stitch or backstitch. Carefully slit the muslin in the centre of the area to be padded, feed in the filling with a bodkin or blunt needle so that you can ease it into any corners, and close up the slit (fig 6).

Patchwork

Patchwork is often used as the basis for quilting. Patchwork developed not least as an economy measure for using up scraps of fabric, but its homely charm led to its development into a stylish craft. Used in conjunction with quilting, the patterns made by the arrangement of patches can be the basis of the sewing line so that each patch has a contoured shape. This helps to show up the selection of both pattern and fabric.

In some areas, especially North America, patchwork quilting became something of a social activity, particularly at 'quilting bees' where women gathered to practise their craft. Designs peculiar to a region evolved, and books setting out examples of these are worth exploring.

Before embarking on anything elaborate, it is best to start with a pattern of simple squares, rectangles or hexagons. You can get metal master shapes or templates from craft shops.

Window templates are useful for laying over a patterned fabric so that you can see the exact area that will show, such as a centred flower. The outer edge of the template will be the edge of the seam allowance (fig 1).

The character of the patchwork will depend to a large extent on the fabrics you choose and the way you arrange the different colours and textures. It is best to use fabrics of a similar weight, and to avoid stretchy or easily frayed ones. If you plan to wash the quilt remember to keep to washable and colourfast materials.

First cut several pieces of card to the exact shape and size of the template. Place each individual card on a piece of fabric of a suitable size and trim the fabric to give a 1 cm overhang all round (fig 2). Turn the edges of the fabric over, and tack them down to the card. At the corners, pleat the fabric neatly (fig 3). When you have a few shapes ready, begin to join them together,

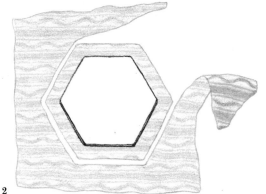

2

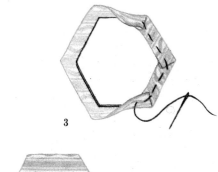

3

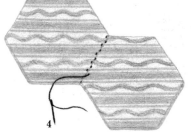

4

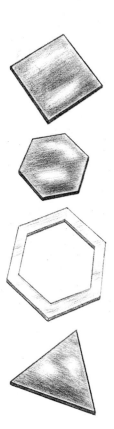

1 *Patchwork templates. The third one down is a window template, useful for centring motifs in the fabric.*

2 *Cut round ordinary templates to give a 1 cm overhang.*

3 *Tack the fabric to the card, pleating the excess at the corners.*

4 *Slipstitch the patches together*

5 *or use herringbone stitch if you won't be quilting the work.*

6 *Sew a set of half-shapes to give the work a straight edge.*

edge to edge. Slipstitch them together finely, avoiding catching up the cardboard in the sewing (fig 4). Make sure that the ends of the thread are secured by sewing backwards for a couple of stitches. For a fancier effect you could use herringbone stitch if you are not intending to quilt the finished patchwork (fig 5).

It is easiest to sew small clusters of patches together and then join the clusters at the end to form the overall design. Press the work on the wrong side, then on the right side, still with the cards in place so that the turnings don't leave a mark. Then snip through the tacking and remove the cards.

If you have used a hexagonal or other non-right-angled shape, you may have to sew a set of several half-shapes in order to end up with a straight edge (fig 6). You could then enclose the edge in a border as described for quilted work (see page 138). Alternatively you could mount the work on a plain fabric and then deal with the edges in the same way, or go on to work the patchwork into a quilt.

5

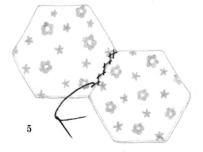

6

Index